LIBRARY ORIENTATION SERIES

edited by Sul H. Lee

PLANNING AND DEVELOPING A LIBRARY ORIENTATION PROGRAM

Proceedings of the Third Annual Conference on
Library Orientation for Academic Libraries,
Eastern Michigan University, May 3-4, 1973

Managing Editor

Mary Bolner

Director, Project LOEX
Eastern Michigan University

Published for the
Center of Educational Resources,
Eastern Michigan University
by

Pierian Press

ANN ARBOR, MICHIGAN
1975

Library of Congress Catalog Card No. 75-676
ISBN 0-87650-061-0

PIERIAN PRESS
P.O. Box 1808
Ann Arbor, Michigan 48106

Contents

Introduction

As the title of this volume indicates, the Third Annual Conference on Library Orientation for Academic Libraries (May 3 and 4,
1973, Eastern Michigan University) was devoted to methods of developing orientation and instruction programs for academic libraries.
The conference was planned as a series of group discussions in which
ideas and experiences could be freely exchanged. The result was a
two-day brainstorming session. Participants described their own
programs (actual or planned), commented on those of others, and
raised many more questions than could be answered in such a short
period of time.

Several themes ran throughout the disucssions. The first involved the use of the terms *orientation* and *instruction*. Although
the distinction between the two was repeatedly pointed out at the
beginning of the discussions, the term *orientation* was generally
used subsequently to include all forms of instruction in library use,
from the most elementary to the most advanced. A second theme
was the need for thorough planning of all aspects of the program.
A third was the interrelationship of all parts of the program and the
fact that the various elements cannot be considered in isolation.
The emphasis on planning and on the development of faculty cooperation which appeared in all the discussions are two examples. The
wedding of methods and materials is another. The fourth theme
involved the fact that the varying situations of different libraries
require tailor-made programs.

One theme that was notably lacking (except in those discussions dealing specifically with it) was evaluation. This is one area
in which librarians in general appear to be very ill at ease and it is an
area that needs much work.

Many people are deserving of gratitude for the role they played
in the preparation of these proceedings: the one-hundred-plus participants who provided the content; the fifteen discussion leaders,
each of whom edited the transcript of his or her group discussion;
and the five discussion leaders who consolidated the edited tran-

scripts into the first five of the following chapters.

It is the hope of all of us involved in the preparation of this volume that it will provide a stimulus to further research in the field of academic library orientation and instruction.

Mary Bolner

Ypsilanti, Michigan
April 14, 1974

GETTING STARTED:

DESIGNING A PROGRAM, PROPOSAL WRITING, FUNDING: A CONVERSATION

Ann Andrew

Discussion Leaders:
Mary Bolner Butterfield, Eastern Michigan University
Lucy Greene, University of Western Ontario
Ann Andrew, Eastern Michigan University

The purpose of a conference such as this one is to gather people together and provide them with a forum for sharing ideas and experiences. For the next hour we're going to be concerned with methods of starting an orientation and instruction program. Some of us have already been through this process, others are just beginning it, and still others are somewhere in the midst of it.

A FABLE

I'm going to tell you a story (completely fictitious, of course) to illustrate the "getting started" process followed at one academic library.

Once upon a time, not too long ago and in a land not too far away, there was a University Library Kingdom. This Library had been doing orientation on an informal basis for a long, long time – mostly things like conducted tours and a few lectures to classes. Then one day the King of the Library had a great idea: Why not expand and formalize the program in order to reach more students more effectively and maybe even get a few clams from the Emperor of Library Resources to run the whole show? When he couldn't think of any reason why not, he whipped out his quill pen and a clean sheet of parchment. At the top of the sheet he wrote "Proposal." Underneath that he wrote down all of his ideas. When he was finished he presented the whole thing to the Citizens of the Library Kingdom (also known as Librarians). They all studied the Proposal very carefully and called a big meeting to discuss it. The First Librarian said, "Well, I don't think we can do X and Y; but we can certainly do Z." The Second Librarian said, "Let's do Q instead." The Third Librarian said, "Well, this really looks pretty nice, but I have a question: Who is going to do it, and how? And to whom are we going to do it?" And the Fourth Librarian said, "Oh, I don't think the Faculty Kingdom is going to like this." After the

1

discussion had gone on like this for a while, the King and a group of his Closest Advisors retired to the Throne Room to discuss the discussion and decide what to do. What they did was rewrite the Proposal. And rewrite it again. Three or four times they rewrote it. While they were rewriting, discussions continued within the Library Kingdom with the Citizens contributing their ideas how and/ or how not to do it. They also consulted with the Citizens of the Faculty Kingdom and the University Administration Kingdom. What they didn't do, however, was spend very much time studying what the recipients of the proposed program (Citizens of the Student Kingdom) needed or wanted, or much time in preliminary planning of precisely how the program would actually work. You see, they were in a terrific hurry to get the Proposal finished and submitted in time to be eligible for some of those clams. Finally, after many gruelling hours of work which resulted in quite a few new gray hairs and the consumption of enormous amounts of Maalox and Alka Seltzer, they came up with something that satisfied nearly everyone in the Library Kingdom. They submitted their Proposal to the King of the University Administration and the Emperor of Library Re--sources, both of whom liked it so much they said, "We'll give you fifty clams to do it." Well, you'd think the King and the Citizens of the Library Kingdom would rejoice at the news, but they didn't. For alas, their program required seventy--five clams. So, it was back to the drawing board (or rather, the Throne Room) for the King and his Advisors. After many more hours of work, more gray hair, more Maalox and Alka Seltzer, they finally came up with a Proposal that pleased all the people it had to please and cost only fifty clams. Shortly thereafter, they got their clams and the new program went into effect and everyone lived happily (or at least, relatively happily) ever after.

Looking back on their experiences, the librarians involved in the above story reached the conclusion that there must be a less harrow--ing way to get an orientation and instruction program started. What kinds of experiences have you had or are you having? What advice would you give to others just beginning the "getting started" process?

DEFINITIONS

It is important at the beginning to give some consideration to the meaning of the terms *orientation* and *instruction*. There is a tendency to lump these together. Certainly they relate, they over--lap, and one is important to the other, but there is a difference. The difference will be critically evident in the materials and methods re--

2

quired to implement the programs. The ultimate implication is financial.

Library orientation refers to helping people feel aware of and comfortable with the building and the services available, with the location of collections, and with the people who service those collections. This is the first level and must precede the second level in user education which we have come to term *library instruction.* The first level, or general orientation, should be very efficiently handled in order that time and energy can be dedicated to instruction. Elementary things such as adequate and effective signs in the library must be considered. If people can easily help themselves, there is a great saving in time and energy and, therefore, money.

FUNDING

The library in the story got a Council on Library Resources grant. I wonder if anybody else thought of getting outside funding for whatever kind of program they started.

We have a graduate reference assistant program that is funded by the Council and the National Endowment for the Humanitites. This is a matching--fund grant where CLR and NEH put up half and the university puts up half.

Do we have to say that we need outside funding?

No, not at all. That's just one source. Funds may be available within the university.

I think that is really important. We should seek funds within other departments. Sometimes even small amounts, such as providing paper to run things off for your classes, can be contributed by the department you are working with.

At our university a few years ago, the History and Political Science Departments received a large grant. The proposal included the need for increased library services, so consequently, the library received a portion of the grant.

One college reference librarian decided he was going to make a film. There happened to be money floating around in the College of Liberal Arts and Sciences which was designated for speakers who never showed up, so he got hold of this money to make his film. You could call it a grant, but it was actually appropriating money that was not otherwise being used.

When we started our lecture program we decided we wanted a slide collection to go with it. We thought we would have to go outside the university for funding because, considering the poverty state of our school, we were sure we'd never be able to get it inside. But we found out that there were means available within the university. For instance, we have a Committee on Improvement of Instruction that provides funding for programs of university—wide interest. So you might look within the university to see if there are any special agencies that will provide money.

There may also be a university research office that will help you seek out sources of outside funds, if that's the way you want to go, and help you write your proposal.

What you really need to do before applying for funding is planning and writing it all down in a proposal. We need to talk about how we are going to get started with planning.

GATHERING SUPPORT

In the Kingdom in the story, all the librarians had the common goal of starting an orientation program. They may have been interested in different aspects of it, but nevertheless, they were all interested. What do you do in a situation where you have one department interested in starting it and you have scattered sympathies among the rest of the staff, but you have an administration which is a bit difficult and taking a wait—and—see attitude? A wait—and—see attitude is no good, because you really can't start anything when they're too busy waiting to see. So what would you do?

In the story, of course, the idea, the stimulus, came from the King (the administration). But in your situation the idea came from somewhere else. Wherever the idea comes from, you have to go around and drum up support. When the idea comes from the top, of course, it's a lot easier to get support. Any suggestions on how to get administration support?

It's hopeless.

It takes initiative. If you're trying to get an outside grant or conjure up some source of funds, you have to show a program or something you're planning to do in the future.

THE INITIAL PLANNING

The initial thinking must take into consideration several factors: What kind of community are you dealing with? What kind of previous library experience do the members of this community bring with them? Will our program be planned with the idea of enticing people into the library or will we concentrate on those who already are coming to the library? The answers to these questions will in great measure determine how you expend your energy in planning and designing a program.

I come from a large institution, and we are ending up having to make two proposals, one outside of the library and one inside the library. We are writing a proposal to the university to schedule an instruction program. Because we have a big library, we have to write another proposal to request support within the library. Without the back up, we can't do it. We are proposing that technical services librarians be released, on a voluntary basis, to assist in giving lecture–tours. In our university, evaluations of librarians include an evaluation of their teaching. It does make it easier for them if they really are doing some teaching.

I wonder if people see a need for writing a proposal. We did and I think it helped us define our goals as well as get extra funding. But maybe a written proposal isn't always necessary.

I think that one thing people can do is write down some objec–tives. Our college is very much into behavioral objectives. In fact, I think we've gone overboard. We don't do anything now without be–havioral objectives. But it has made us really look at what we are doing. An actual proposal wasn't necessary because any extra money was totally impossible.

So in other words, you can use a part of the proposal.

Yes, I really think the behavioral objectives now are absolutely necessary.

It also helps faculty see what you are doing.

It seems to me that one of the problems the people in the story had was that they didn't thoroughly plan the thing before they started writing the proposal. They didn't have any idea where they wanted to go before they started. What planning should they have done?

I think we better find out what the needs are. You have to talk with faculty and students. Contact them to find out what they want. We may have an idea, but we may also be out in left field.

Right. Those are the key things when you're getting started.

USER SURVEYS

How do you contact the students? What do you do?

Perhaps some kind of a survey. We have tried to evaluate the effects of our graduate reference assistant program. We have a poll every spring, taking every tenth student, sending them a very brief questionnaire asking how much they use the library, whether they have consulted reference librarians, whether they have consulted the reference assistants, etc. It takes two follow–ups to get any measur–able results.

Did you contact anyone in your sociology department for help, or did you just do your own questionnaire?

We contacted the sociology department. You have to work with somebody who knows how to do it. We had the bright idea of standing on the college green and asking people as they passed by, and they said, "No, no, no, you've got to do it scientifically . . . . "

I'm not too sure that the way to determine what students don't know about the library is to ask the students. If someone would come up to me and ask me what I don't know about national biblio-graphies, I would be hard put to answer. I might know something, but I might not know what I don't know. I think one thing we shouldn't overlook is the ability of the reference librarians to observe shortcomings on the part of the student. It's an exhibited need rather than a felt need, possibly.

You've got to document it, that's the problem. The survey technique provides you with something you can use for documen-tation. It makes it all more valid.

I am wondering how many people have made surveys of their users. We are going to have a sample survey this summer and we have a very diversified population.

How do you make a sample survey?

We formed a committee. Initially there were two people, and it has increased to eight. A brain storming session determined what we wanted to find out. We sat in a conference room, threw ideas out, then organized them into categories, such as collection related, physical layout, information regarding materials, services, etc. We ended up with hundreds of questions but sorted them into eight basic questions which were divided into four or five parts. We took the advice of experts and planned a brief questionnaire. It shouldn't take more than five minutes to answer.

How will you distribute these questionnaires?

We will hand them out to people for one week as they come into the library.

Do you feel this will be a true random sample?

It will not be a random sample of the total population, but a sample of those who come into the library. We have identified that as a problem at the outset.

For whatever encouragement it may be, our library system just completed a user survey. The subject of the survey was user reaction to a new building as well as to services provided. The usual kinds of questions were included: Why did you come into the library? How long do you stay? How frequently do you come? Do you find the services helpful? What is your reaction to a new building, the lighting, the furniture, etc.? As an afterthought a computer program was developed to manipulate the findings. If we were doing it again, I think the questionnaire would be designed in such a way that it would be machine scannable and manipulable.

Most universities probably do an analysis of their student pop-ulation through their admissions office. I am from a small school and am lucky enough to have access to this information. I wonder if anyone else has access to admissions data?

I am from a community college and have full access to anything I ask admissions for. However, we did a survey in which we asked about students' reading level, the number of years they had been out of high school, and the kind of background they had in high school. We distributed the questionnaire in the English classes figuring that we would get a representative sample there since most people in our community college do take English at one time or another.

I am also at a college where freshmen must take English in their first or second semester. Through the English Department we found that a great segment of the students did not know the *Readers' Guide.* As a result, we are aiming at that portion of the student population which needs very elementary instruction.

We approach this question a little differently. A library use test is given in combination with a variety of other tests during orientation week. It takes about five minutes to complete. We identify all students who score 6 or less out of the 12-question test. The test is de-signed to identify those who are not familiar with the information on a catalog card or are not able to use the *Readers' Guide.* We feel if students can do these two things, they can at least begin to function in the library. If they can't, they need help right away. We follow up with three sets of exercises which take about half an hour each.

What are the personnel requirements of your program?

We use three or four librarians for an hour or two during the first few weeks of classes. The program is staged. After the students have become familiar with the *Readers' Guide* and the card catalog, they are introduced to the *Social Sciences and Humanities Index,* the *Essay and General Literature Index,* the Library of Congress subject headings book, etc.

Do you intend to have a follow-up survey on the attitudes of the students to this type of program?

We are talking about it.

That brings up a comment I read recently about a survey of engineering students at a technological institute. One of the questions asked was, "Do you want to learn how to use the library?" Sixty-two percent answered no.

Even on a small scale, when you begin a new orientation or in-struction program, should it grow out of what the students are work-ing on at the time, from their problems or assignments, or can you go in with your own separate program?

Well, the freshmen I have come to campus about a week before the upperclassmen, and I present the basic orientation then. Later, in their freshman composition classes, I work with the professor and what he or she is doing in the class. Some of them are working on plays, some on fiction, some on topics of current concern, and so on.

So your program began during the freshman orientation period, which was a program you already had going in your university. I think this is an important point to keep in mind when you design a library orientation or instruction program. Build on what's there. For example, if you have faculty that are already sort of library conscious, you can use faculty in your program. Otherwise you would have a lot of work to do in building a program utilizing faculty cooperation.

I believe we have hit on a point that is important, and I'm not sure that we have completely answered it. You may have an idea for developing a program, but is it an isolated idea that you are imposing on somebody, or is it in response to an expressed need that you have identified?

That's a good question for everyone to consider.

I think the thing to avoid is just making up your own assump-- tions of what is needed and plodding along with the program whether or not it's in accordance with what the faculty are doing or with what the students are interested in.

This is how we've tried to plan our program. We found that even before various classes were scheduled to come to the library, they had a need for basic things like index location and use, and where the periodicals are, and so on. So we scheduled tours during freshman orientation week.

We had an experience doing that and discovered that if you try this before the students feel motivated, it turns into a disaster.

Right. We don't try to give any instruction then, just show them around, and create an image.

FACULTY SUPPORT

We've found that our most successful programs grew out of classroom needs. They came from those teachers who were library conscious. They felt the need for instruction, and they were our best support. On the other hand there were some teachers who did not feel that way about it. They seemed to think that you were wasting their time, that they had subject matter to cover, and that the library instruction slowed them down. It has always baffled me as to how you can convince the faculty -- maybe you never can -- that in order for the students to be really successful, there is a great need for them to know how to use resources.

When I contacted all the professors and offered to give library instruction, I had one professor say, "No, my students don't need it." Then when these students started coming in asking questions like "What's the *Readers' Guide?*", I started asking "Whose class are you in?" I kept track, and now I have been able to say for a fact that these students need the instruction, and the professors are starting to call on me when they give a library assignment.

We have a program that is kind of a back door approach. It's called Current Awareness, and it involves working directly with faculty members. The reference librarians who have various specializations are assigned to different departments to contact the faculty there asking: What are your research needs? What courses are you teaching? Which journals do you currently read? Which would you like to be kept informed about? We establish such a profile for each faculty member. Then we inform them about new books as they arrive, and we xerox the tables of contents from periodicals which interest them. We've established such rapport that they are now coming to us with library assignments.

I think you are bringing up another main point that we would want to consider, and that is that your program should be related to the university program. Yours is related through the faculty, through direct faculty contact, so you are relating to the needs of the university.

We are taking a similar approach. We are establishing miniworkshops on topics to introduce different library tools and services. You can have coffee or something to drink, and get acquainted with the faculty who are not normally library users. And when they start talking about their problems, you bring up the kinds of things the library can do. I've also been going to their departments and describing segments of the program.

PERSONNEL

We've been talking about what we're going to do and how to get moral and financial support for it, but what about who's going to do it?

Do you think it's possible to start a program without additional personnel? Just redesign the duties and reschedule librarians in reference or public service? Or do you think it's necessary to have additional personnel?

This is where a plan of action comes in. You have to sit down first and ask: What are we going to need? How are we going to get it? Then you'll have to determine if you can get it without additional personnel or if you can manipulate schedules and work out released time for personnel.

Orientation and instruction activities often fall on the reference department, and this is a logical place. The first wave breaks over us, and we're the ones who are interested in orientation. However, the reference department has a certain number of duties that have to be done, and orientation is expendable, whereas the other duties aren't.

So, if you have a small staff, you don't do orientation. If, at some point, you can convince your director to beef up the reference staff so the minimum duties can be maintained with time left over to devote to orientation, then the program can get started.

How do you handle orientation?

We have a fairly large staff. We have four subject divisions and each one has at least four subject specialists who serve as reference librarians. Prior to 1970, we didn't have special orientation librarians. We have always all chipped in when it was time to give tours, and whenever a faculty member wanted a lecture for a class, the subject specialist for that area would give the lecture. When the program was formalized, we started out with two additional orientation librarians who took over the bulk of the work with freshman courses and coordinated the orientation and instruction activities that the rest of us were doing. The subject specialists or reference librarians continue to help out with tours and give lectures and instruction in their subject areas.

How were the orientation librarians chosen?

They were subject specialists with reference backgrounds and an interest in teaching.

There's a certain problem that's basic to this whole thing. This may sound absurd considering that this is an orientation conference, but if we, as a reference department, become more effective, we may develop a really good orientation program where we now have only an informal one. If we had a real orientation program going, we might get more people in the library and have more business at the reference desk than we could handle.

We have found that the more orientation we do, the less busy we are at the desk. The students are more aware of library resources and are more sophisticated in using the library.

We've found that the more orientation we do, the busier we are at the reference desk. The students seem to be more at ease in seeking assistance and more aware of what the library has to offer.

What about separate courses in library use?

We have separate courses in addition to the regular instruction done by the librarians. We've found that course or assignment-related instruction given in cooperation with the teaching faculty is more effective than the separate course.

SUMMARY

To summarize: We start an orientation and instruction program with an idea and drum up support for it. Then comes a plan of action. We have to decide who is going to receive what kind of instruction and who is going to give it. We have to set objectives and decide

what we want to accomplish and how we're going to accomplish
it. We also have to build an evaluation procedure into the program
so we can determine whether or not we're meeting our objectives.
Evaluation is important for two reasons: First, funding agencies
(the university or college included) want to know what results their
money is producing. And second, the information provided by e-
valuation will indicate how and where the program needs revising.
One thing we didn't get into was the technique of writing the proposal. However, that's something fairly easy to dig out of the lit--
erature. In addition, most funding agencies provide guidelines and
many schools have an office that will provide assistance.

CAMPUS CONTACTS:

DEVELOPING FACULTY COOPERATION
AND CAMPUS PUBLICITY

METHODS AND MATERIALS

Hannelore B. Rader

Discussion Leaders:
Mary George, University of Michigan
Peter Malanchuk, Western Michigan University
Hannelore B. Rader, Eastern Michigan University

The second discussion session, "Campus Contacts . . . ," dealt
with two separate aspects of the library orientation program: Development of faculty cooperation, and publicity of the program.

First of all, it must be stated for the purpose of uniformity that
the term *library orientation* as used within includes the concept of
orienting the user to the library and its resources as well as all phases
of library instruction. Therefore, whenever a reference is made to
library orientation, the term is used in its broadest sense.

FACULTY COOPERATION

Why is librarian--faculty cooperation needed?

In order to realize a successful and effective library orientation
program it is necessary to work closely with the faculty to provide
the motivational factor. Students are usually motivated to learn
because they have to do assignments to finish the course in order to
receive a grade and credit. If the library orientation experience becomes part of the coursework or is needed to complete an assignment, students will be interested, they will attend, and they will have
a learning experience. The person who can make the library orientation experience a part of the coursework is the faculty member.
Through the faculty then, librarians can reach the students to provide them with effective instruction in library resources.

How is faculty cooperation developed?

There are formal and informal ways to contact faculty. Ideally,
at any one institution, both methods can be utilized.

Formal contact is established whenever the administration (both
library and college or university) favors the library orientation program and helps to initiate it. Department heads are contacted either
by phone or mail. The librarian can inform the department head

about the orientation program and can ask to have it publicized within the department in order to solicit cooperation of the other members of the department. The department head may also suggest specific courses (and their instructors) which would benefit from such a program. Furthermore, the librarian may be invited to a department meeting to promote the orientation program.

The personal visit to the department head should be followed by personal visits to individual faculty members who teach courses which incorporate either library research or library assignments. In talking to the faculty members, the orientation program can be outlined and explained and its usefulness for the involved course can be pointed out. At this time it is also possible to plan the library class session with the instructor to help meet his or her instructional objectives.

If the route through the department head is not possible, the librarian can also determine which instructors to contact by studying the course schedule to see which courses include research. Then contact can be made with the instructor of such courses.

It is also possible to work through faculty members who are frequent users of the library even though they may not teach an appropriate course for the library orientation program. However, the librarian could discuss the program with them and they in turn could publicize it to their colleagues.

There is still another method to initiate faculty contact for library orientation. This can occur through activities at the reference desk. Whenever the librarian notices that a number of students ask for help on the same library assignment, he or she can ascertain who the instructor of the course is and thereafter he or she can be contacted to subtly offer library assistance in the form of bibliographic instruction.

Informally, there are also various methods to contact faculty. Librarians can demonstrate their expertise in information science by keeping individual faculty members abreast of new library acquisitions by sending them lists of new books, notices of new reference works, particular articles, etc. This may entice some faculty members to call the librarian or to visit the library and at this time the librarian has a chance to inform the faculty member about library services, particularly the instructional services.

Other informal ways of contacting faculty have been tried by librarians in various institutions. Some have given an open house in the library with cookies and coffee, some have had wine-tasting parties or beer parties for faculty or even students in the library, others have invited faculty to luncheons. Depending upon the size of the institution and the budget, these social events were limited in some ways, either to a department or to new faculty.

Another effective way to develop faculty contact is for the

librarians to achieve greater visibility on campus. If they can become members of the faculty senate and university committees, they will have a chance to inform faculty members about library services and at the same time they will be able to demonstrate their usefulness as members of the university community because of their committee involvement. This committee work can prove extremely useful in promoting the library's instructional services to faculty. Faculty contact can also be established through the librarian's professional involvement in a subject area. For example: The education librarian could join educational associations and go with other faculty members to conferences and workshops offered by these associations.

Some librarians have also had success with library workshops for faculty. Often these are for new faculty to acquaint them with the library resources. However, these workshops have also been used to introduce newly acquired reference sets, new library technology or new library services to faculty. After thus informing the instructors, many times an invitation to their classes will follow.

How is faculty cooperation maintained?

After the initial contact with a faculty member has been made, the librarian has to make sure the contact is maintained and utilized for the library instruction program. It helps here to keep a record of each instructor's research interest and to send him or her notices of new materials on this subject received in the library. It is also necessary to renew the contact with the faculty member each term or semester to remind him or her of the library's instructional service.

If the instructor has indicated that he or she would like the librarian to provide bibliographic instruction for the course, the librarian and the instructor must then plan the library instruction together. This usually involves the classification of the research assignment, topics involved, sources to be suggested, the librarian's preparation of any bibliographic aids or guides such as pathfinders, and perhaps even the method of presenting the information such as team teaching, demonstration or audio–visual equipment. The librarian should also encourage the instructor to be present during the library session. This is important because it encourages the student's interest and usually provides the instructor with much new information and makes him or her realize the need for this library instruction.

PROBLEMS IN DEVELOPING FACULTY COOPERATION

If the librarians do not have faculty status, it will be harder for them to establish faculty contact. They will not be able to work through the faculty senate or university committees. They might also have to work harder to prove themselves as instructors to teaching faculty.

If the library and--or university administration does not en--courage library orientation, librarians interested in promoting this will have to do it as an added duty. They will be severely limited in time and resources under those conditions.

If the curriculum does not include many courses which incor--porate library research, librarians will be limited in how much biblio--graphic instruction they can provide.

Some faculty members may view the library orientation session provided by the librarians as a convenient time--off for themselves. In some cases faculty members have interpreted the librarian's offer to assist in research instruction as an offer to prepare 30 or more paper bibliographies for their classes.

If only one or two librarians are responsible for developing faculty cooperation, they must be careful to involve other librarians in order to avoid "empire building."

OTHER PROGRAM PUBLICITY

Much of the program publicity is, of course, accomplished through the individual faculty contact. If the presentation of the library orientation session was well done both the students and faculty members will promote it. This is the most effective type of publicity. A faculty member hearing about the library's instruction--al service through a colleague will usually utilize the service too, if at all possible.

Students who appreciate the library instruction session may tell their friends about it, who in turn may pressure an instructor into incorporating a library instruction session if there is a related assign--ment.

Some libraries have also offered term paper clinics, research paper assistance, mini--courses in the library or formal courses in li--brary research to students, either on a voluntary basis or for credit. Some of these offerings have met with success, others not.

In some situations students are trained to assist other students in the library. Usually these are graduate library science students who work closely with a librarian in preparing guides, bibliographies, and who assist with reference work or even library orientation. These students can often communicate better with other students and they will also advertise the service to others.

Librarians can also contact student groups and organizations on campus to offer instruction in finding information for whatever they need, coursework or personal.

Student representation on library committees can also help to publicize the library's services and to create an awareness of the li--

brary's role in education.

Publicizing the library orientation program can also be done through the campus radio and TV stations, newspaper, any student or faculty news letters, or meetings of faculty and students.

Librarians can also try to ascertain students' interests and offer them a place in the library where they can browse through materials of interest, where they can see a film program, have a discussion, or hear lectures on these interests.

CONCLUSION

It was established that librarian--faculty cooperation is necessary for a successful library orientation program. This cooperation is de-- veloped in three stages – initial contact, planning the librarian's par- ticipation in the classroom, and maintaining the faculty contact. Methods of developing faculty cooperation were discussed and prob- lem areas identified. Other methods to publicize the library orien- tation program were also discussed. Available services on campus should be utilized such as radio, TV, newspapers and other publi- cations. Contact should also be established with students, either individually through the reference desk and committees, or through groups and organizations. Throughout the discussion it was apparent that the development of campus contacts would require constant effort on the part of librarians. It would also require time, energy, patience and a love for all mankind.

THE POSITION OF THE ORIENTATION PROGRAM WITHIN THE LIBRARY

James E. Ward

Discussion Leaders:
George Gardiner, Oakland University
Cecily Little, Central Michigan University
James E. Ward, David Lipscomb College

It was appropriate that the topic, "The Position of the Orien –tation Program Within the Library," be selected as one of the early considerations in discussing the implementation of a library instruction program, since basic to the success of any program is the po--sition it will occupy in the total setting -- not only its place admin-istratively, but the place it holds in the collective thought of the en-tire library staff as well as the academic community.

One of the difficulties in the various discussion groups was the clarification of terminology, particularly in regard to the term *li-brary orientation.* Was it to be considered in the narrow sense of a special subset of the library's instructional program, involving an acquaintance of users with a resource and not instruction in the use of that resource? Or was it to be construed in the more general sense of the entire instructional program itself, comprehending both teach--ing about the resources in the library and also teaching the use of these resources? The general consensus seemed to favor the latter, so it is with that connotation that library orientation will be discussed in the report for this session.

Although there was a wide range of topics discussed by the three groups, there were many which tended to be common to all. Therefore, for the purpose of these proceedings, those ideas which are pertinent to the assigned subject have been consolidated under the general heading of "Basic Considerations in Determining the Po-sition of the Orientation Program Within the Library," as follows:

TYPE OF INSTITUTION

One of the factors to consider when planning a library orien-tation program is the type of institution in which it will operate. Is it planned for a large university, with extensive graduate programs? Is it for an undergraduate college only? A junior or community college? A professional school? Vocational? Although there are characteristics common to all library orientation programs, they will be more effective when tailored to meet the needs of the local setting. Moreover, the type of institution will, in all likelihood, place obvious limitations on the type of program which can be planned.

The conference included particpants representing most of the above types of institutions, ranging from small undergraduate colleges to the very large universities. Represented also were junior and community colleges. However, no pattern regarding the position of the library orientation program seemed to emerge which could clearly be identified with any particular type or size of institution. Institutional factors, however, which did seem to influence the program most often, at least indirectly, were related to the overall attitude toward the library throughout the campus by administration, faculty, and students and the support given the library program, both financially and otherwise. Furthermore, the relationship which existed between the library personnel and the above groups tended to have a tremendous effect on the library orientation program -- not only on its placement within the library, but on whether or not it even existed to any appreciable degree. Important, too, was the extent to which the library program is included in the overall objectives of the college or university in which it operates.

THE STUDENTS

The students for whom library orientation is planned certainly are one of the basic considerations affecting the type of program as well as its placement. Today's college population arrives with varied backgrounds in library usage, ranging from those who have had little or no exposure to libraries to students who have had extensive instruction in library usage in their pre--college training. This compounds the problem for the college library in trying to plan a program which will meet the needs of all students. Therefore, the background and level of sophistication in library skills must be considered in charting such a program.

Concern was expressed regarding the type of library orientation programs to plan for the large universities where both undergraduate and graduate students often share library facilities, and whether or not there should be separate programs of instruction. If the program is aimed primarily at the undergraduate, as some suggested, this might be unfair to those graduate students who have come from institutions which did not provide good library orientation. Although undergraduate students might be the primary focus of the library's effort to overcome their lack of skill and self--confidence in using the library, there seemed to be general agreement that the library also has a definite responsibility to graduate students, and even faculty members, who feel the need for library orientation and that an effort should be made to begin where the users are and make an attempt to assist them in their growth toward independent use of the materials.

Enrollment alone often appeared to be a limiting factor in planning a workable library orientation program, since many of the participants reported difficulty in reaching the enormous populations on the larger campuses with present staff and facilities. Further, an influencing factor was the housing pattern on the campus, since the type of program may be dictated to some degree by whether or not most of the students live on or near the campus or if they are pre-dominantly commuters – particularly where night classes are in-volved.

THE LIBRARY

The position, as well as the type of library orientation program, will be affected somewhat by the library itself, including the physical facilities, location on campus, its stated objectives, and the col-lection.

Some of the participants represented campuses with only one central library, whereas others came from institutions having multiple facilities, including separate graduate and undergraduate buildings as well as numerous departmental libraries, the latter requiring greater coordination and, in most cases, more personnel in providing ad-equate instruction in use of collections which are decentralized, but with an obvious advantage when employing course–related instruc-tion.

There was general agreement that the library should have written objectives, but only a few of the participants indicated that their libraries did, in fact, have such in writing.   226592

Every library should be guided in its program by a set of written objectives or purposes which not only are compatible with the goals of its parent institution but are carefully planned and understood by all members of the staff. If this is done, it is here where the position of the library orientation program within the library should be clear-ly stated. If, as one participant indicated, one of the important ob-jectives of the library is to develop the ability of the students to use the library effectively, then it should occupy an important place in the program and should be included as one of the library's goals. In a well–managed library such an objective, carefully stated, clearly defined, and widely accepted, should find its fulfillment in a well functioning program of efficient implementation.

One last consideration in regard to the library is the collection itself. As the late Millicent Palmer often said, "You can't teach the use of something which the library doesn't have." Therefore, a good library orientation program is contingent on a collection which is adequate to support the curriculum of its parent institution, and if library orientation is to occupy an important and useful place on a campus, it must have access to the materials which are pertinent to the academic areas represented by the students receiving the in-- struction. Otherwise, it is doomed to failure and nonacceptance by faculty and students.

NON--LIBRARY FACULTY

Not to be overlooked in planning library orientation are the non--library faculty members, because it is they who often will be one of the keys to the success or failure of the program. In addition to the administrative personnel and students, it is necessary to have the support, understanding, acceptance, and cooperation of the faculty in the various departments, since they will often be involved -- directly or indirectly -- in library orientation, depending on the nature of the program. Without this type of relationship the most beautifully--designed plan is destined to failure -- or, at best, some-- thing short of what is desirable.

In an attempt to build the above type of relationship between the library and general faculty, every possible effort should be made to convince them that the library in no way is trying to usurp their responsibilities, but, on the contrary, it is trying to supplement what they are doing in the regular classroom. Some participants reported favorable results from team teaching in library orientation involving both the library and non--library faculty members. Such a plan should offer many possibilities.

One means suggested for building a closer relationship with the faculty and obtaining greater involvement was through the faculty library committee, or perhaps a library orientation/instruction committee, where participation not only will bring better under-- standing of the program, but greater acceptance of it on the part of the faculty, as well as the students if they are included on the committee.

NATURE OF THE LIBRARY ORIENTATION PROGRAM

The position of library orientation within the library will be dependent, to a large extent, on the very nature of the program it-- self, and one of the first considerations here is the statement of the objectives of the program. What is the overall purpose of the pro-- gram, and how is this to be achieved? This should be based on and should be determined only after careful study before initiating a program. Objectives must be clearly stated and compatible with those of the library and of the parent institution. A program without such a basic foundation is quite likely to result in chaos and inefficiency, with the end result being possible failure.

So often library orientation programs have sprung up suddenly as a result of one person's interests or to meet a temporary need and have found themselves without purpose, plan, or a place to call home in the library's organizational structure. This, no doubt, has contributed to the lack of consistency in the position of the library orientation program within the library, its placement being determined often by areas of the library where the most interest lies or where the most library orientation--minded personnel are employed. Although there were some differences of opinion on the amount and kind of planning which should be done, it was agreed that programs which are to stand the test of time and effectively serve any worthwhile need must be based on sound planning. This planning should involve a careful study of the local situation to discover the needs and the best methods for meeting them. Such a study conducted by qualified persons and involving a large number of particpants -- including faculty, administration, and students, in addition to library personnel -- should help not only to provide a sensible base from which to build, but to ensure greater participation and acceptance once the program is operational.

Although long--range planning seems more desirable, it was agreed that often short--term programs must be planned to meet emergency situations. However, to provide the continuity and stability which a well--functioning program demands, there should be long--range planning with enough flexibility to provide for adaptations and/or changes when needs and interests demand. Such systematic planning, over the years, will provide the depth and quality which not only will reap greater rewards but should reduce the possibility of a multiplicity of problems developing as the program grows.

Yet, there is little evidence from a study of the literature or a survey of the conference participants that a large number of the present library orientation programs were preceded by the above type of planning, and a good percentage of the ones who have probably are recipients of special grants where such planning was required. Why is this the case? One reason given was the lack of time. Good planning requires time, and this is often a rare commodity in libraries. As stated earlier, often a program begins more or less as a "back pocket" approach to meet an emergency situation and in many cases is done in addition to the regular duties of one or more library staff members, suddenly to discover that it has, like Topsy, grown to an unwieldly size. The result is that often the so--called planning has to be done in "reverse," often requiring considerably more time and effort than would otherwise have been necessary. Another problem here is that only a fraction of the users may be receiving library orientation, whereas systematic planning would guarantee that all students conceivably could be reached, rather than just the ones who created the need.

Repsonses from conference participants indicated that the majority of the library orientation programs in institutions which they represented had begun with very little advance planning and that often there have been disappointing results. One problem has been that there have really been no model programs in college and university libraries which could be used as examples to follow in establishing programs, particularly those which would apply in specific situations without major adaptations. Another reason is the lack of properly-trained personnel in the area of library orientation. Very few of the library schools include library orientation and instruction as part of the curriculum, with the result being that it must be learned elsewhere, often through trial-and-error.

Further, it was suggested that some people are frightened away by lengthy plans, and that it might be preferable to begin small until support is gained, and then the program could expand. Yet, it could be rightly argued that there should be some basic plan -- however large or small.

Some interesting questions emerged in regard to planning: What are we to do if there is a felt need for library orientation and yet no time for the planning mentioned above? Are we to "shelve" our program until time and personnel allow such planning? Then, too, what happens to the students during the time of planning? Although most participants agreed that often the "back pocket" emergency approach is sometimes necessary and that often it must be used to some extent during the planning period, it seemed to be the general consensus that library orientation is more likely to be effective in achieving the objectives of a well-grounded program, on a long-range basis, if it is preceded by a period of careful, systematic planning.

The position of library orientation in the library, in all probability, will be influenced by the stimulus for its initiation. A Reference Department-based program may have started as the result of certain problems at the reference desk (e.g., repetition of the same questions, which cannot be handled on an individual basis; difficulty in use of certain materials; location questions, etc.), with the realization that traditional reference service does not meet the real needs of students in assignments involving their library research any more than merely answering questions at the reference desk. Or, it may be that members of the reference staff have heard the familiar expression, "The library doesn't have anything on my subject," when the real problem was that the student did not know how to find the materials.

The origin of the library orientation program may be in the Circulation Department, because the very strategy of its location places these personnel in a position to spot student problems in use of the library. It may even develop from an effort of the Circulation Department to reverse a trend in decreasing circulation figures – a statistic which has questionable value by many.

Library orientation may originate with the director of the library, who is convinced of the need for a program by pressures from various segments of the faculty or student body or who, as one participant pointed out, is influenced by the low level use of the library by students and is prompted to do something about it. Or, it could well be that the director originates the idea because of his or her interest in library instruction as a means of helping the library to better fill its role as the heart of the academic community.

The program may start from interest generated by the students, themselves, or perhaps from the non--library faculty or faculty library committee. Again, in these cases, its placement would depend on the judgment of the director of the library, hopefully with the help of the staff.

An important fact to keep in mind is that often the origin of the idea for initiation of a library orientation program may be influential in determining the place it will occupy, not only in the library – physically and otherwise -- but throughout the campus, and the greater the amount of enthusiasm generated for the program, the greater the chances are that it will be widely accepted.

Another important factor to consider is the type of program planned. Is it merely setting up tours for freshmen and transfer students? Does it involve giving bibliographic lectures to advanced classes in specific subject areas? Is it an instructional program, per--haps a formal one which involves giving credit? Is it an outreach program where the staff is involved a great deal in trying to go out and develop interest among faculty members so that they might encourage their students to come into the library and learn how to use the materials? Do you plan to use computer--assisted instruction? Self--instruction? Answers to these questions will have a definite effect on the place which the library orientation program occupies, since many of the above will require, in addition to qualified personnel, an organizational structure which is compatible with specific techniques of instruction.

One of the most important considerations in determining the place of library orientation in the library is the person or persons who are responsible for conducting it. It was discovered that libraries represented at the conference had programs ranging from separate departments with full--time library orientation librarians to programs which were just in the planning stages, with no specific person given the responsibility for library orientation. The majority of the participants, however, fell somewhere between these two extremes and reported a miscellany of structures insofar as orga--nizations and personnel were concerned.

As indicated, one plan reported was a separate department within the library for library orientation, with personnel given full--time responsibility for planning and conducting the program under the direction of a library orientation librarian, who is directly re--sponsible to the director of the library. For obvious reasons, few participants reported this type of plan, since few libraries have sufficient staff and budget to support such a program. This plan would have the advantage of allowing sufficient time to plan and conduct the program without the pressures of other duties which compete with time and attention.

Some conference participants reported the use of library orien--tation committees, composed only of library personnel in some cases, or others which included representatives from the non--library faculty and student body. Usually this committee served primarily as an advisory group to the library orientation personnel and assisted in planning and in communications between the library and the aca--demic community. It was suggested that in order to make the com--mittee more effective and to avoid some of the problems which had developed from arbitrary assignment, members should be appointed on the basis of their interest and/or ability in library orientation and, wherever possible, to represent a cross section of the groups involved. It is possible that the responsibility of such a committee might be combined with those of the faculty library committee, if such exists.

The majority of plans reported were conducted as a part of the Public Services Area, the most frequent being an auxiliary unit of the Reference Department or occasionally the Circulation Department. Some reported the use of student library assistants, clerical personnel, and library technical assistants in library orientation as an effort to involve as many of the staff as possible and since many of them work in areas where they are aware of readers' confusion, needs, gaps in knowledge, etc., often long before the library faculty. Further, it was felt that this would create the feeling of being a part of the team, that library orientation should really be a team effort, and that every person who works in the Public Services Area should be able to assist a student. It is not likely that a library orientation person can be available at all hours, so if others in the Public Services Area are familiar with the program, this not only will relieve the library orien--

26

tation staff, but will, in all likelihood, eventuate in a more effective program. If it is true here, as one participant suggested, that the large majority of the questions at the reference desk do not require professional training, then it seems a wiser use of personnel to utilize paraprofessionals and others wherever appropriate and thereby free professionally--trained persons for other duties. One problem mentioned here was that often student assistants or paraprofessional personnel attempt to give help for which they aren't trained and may assume that they know more than they do after a small amount of training. Yet, with a well--planned program this could be avoided through a good system of periodic in--service training, with emphasis on referral of difficult questions, etc. to proper personnel. This training could also be supplemented through the use of handbooks and other materials.

It seemed to be the general feeling of the groups that irregardless of the organizational pattern used, responsibility for library orientation should be clearly defined and that this be understood by all persons involved, including the library staff, the administration, students, and non--library faculty, thus eliminating the possibility of conflicts or rivalry among individuals or departments which might be involved in the program. Opinion was somewhat divided regarding the desirability of a separate department for library orientation, but there was general agreement that the responsibility should be centered on one person, regardless of title, whose main job is to plan, coordinate, and direct the program. Whether in a separate department or a part of another area, he or she should be given sufficient personnel, budget, cooperation, support, and time to permit the accomplishment of the purposes for which the program was designed.

The place of the library orientation program is dependent somewhat on the background and history of such programs in the library for which it is planned. When initiating a program in a college with no previous library orientation, one might encounter fewer difficulties than where a program is already in operation or has been at some time in the past, since often it may be necessary to overcome certain prejudices and/or traditions of the faculty, students, and perhaps other members of the library staff. Therefore, it is important to understand the history of library orientation in a particular institution before embarking on a program.

LIBRARY STAFF

The discussants also seemed to favor a plan which would involve as many of the library staff as possible. In most libraries there are persons with the expertise needed in various phases of the library orientation program, and it was felt that these persons should also be included in some capacity. Not only would this improve the quality of the program, but it could be a means of uniting the staff in a common effort for the good of the library and its users.

The political situation in the library will determine to a large extent the possibility of broad involvement in such cross–departmental programs. It is important to know the general opinion of the entire staff regarding library orientation. Do they favor it? Can you depend on their help? Are departments insular, or do you have a staff which has good and close relationships? Are there persons on the staff with experience or interest in library orientation?

Often one of the most difficult obstacles to overcome when initiating a new program is the library staff itself, and, no doubt, all library personnel will not be warm toward library orientation and in-struction. Yet, without widespread support among the library personnel, the program is not likely to be as effective as it could be with general acceptance. Therefore, it seems desirable, particularly in small libraries, to make an attempt to gain acceptance by all members of the staff, and even though all do not participate directly, a sympathetic attitude toward the program and a reasonably good understanding of it will heighten the chances of overall success. Particularly is this important with personnel in the Public Services Area, where much of the contact with users occurs. The above type of feeling is more likely to occur when a large number of the staff have been involved in planning the program. It was generally agreed that, although the major burden rests with persons who are given major responsibility for library orientation, personnel in the various departments within the library should be called on to assist wherever interest, training, expertise, desire, and time are sufficient to justify and whenever approval for such participation is granted by the library administration. As suggested, if library personnel expect to have faculty status and equate themselves with other faculty, then serious consideration should be given by *all* the staff to the teaching function of librarians.

This leads us to a discussion of the director of the library and his or her relationship to the library orientation program. A considerable amount of time was spent in disucssing the attitude of the director toward, and the role he or she should play, in library orientation. It was suggested by some that the director is the key person in determining the success of the program and that without his or her active support it is doomed to failure. The word "active" is important, because lukewarmness or indifference on the part of the director might do more harm to the program than his or her syaing "No."

In most cases it will be an advantage to the program to have the support of the director, since in all probability other members of the library staff are more likely to favor a program which had administrative approval.

How does one gain approval and support from the director? In reply to this question which was posed by one participant, it was suggested that if the director of the library does not recognize the need for library orientation or has varying opinions on how it should be done, one should not give up. With patience one may convince the director that such a program is worth considering. It is even possible that support might be mustered from students, from non-library faculty, or even other members of the library staff which, in turn, would influence the firector to change his or her position. Here again, careful planning is important, since today's library administrators are expecting something more than the personal whims of one or more people when adding new programs and additional costs, and rightly should expect such a program to be justified in terms of need, cost–effectiveness, etc.

It was pointed out, however, that more than administrative support is required in order to implement and conduct a good program of library orientation, and that even with the director's support it is necessary to have competent personnel to plan and coordinate the program, since few administrators will have the time for direct involvement in the program.

A question also was raised regarding the source of training for library orientation personnel. As mentioned earlier, few library schools include this topic in their curricula, and there are few established programs in operation which can be used as models for techniques of instruction, materials, etc. Therefore, in most cases it has been necessary to learn through trial--and--error, particularly for library personnel who do not have training and experience as teachers in other fields of study. This points out the need for more extensive in--service education at the local level, as well as additional growth through the various types of continuing education provided at conferences, workshops, etc.

As would be expected, one of the major problems given by participants was the lack of time for planning and conducting library orientation. The majority of the attendants at the conference reported programs in which personnel devoted only part–time to library orientation, and in many cases it was an added responsibility to an already full--time position. As long as this situation continues the progress of library orientation, no doubt, will be stymied. Some means must be found to provide sufficient time for library orientation, either for full--time personnel or with released time from other duties in order to conduct a high quality program. One answer to the problem may be, as implied earlier, the sharing of personnel from the various departments in the library, but again this should not be done as an extra duty, but released time should be provided to devote specifically to library orientation.

FINANCIAL SUPPORT

It is important that no attempt be made to sell library orienta--tion as an inexpensive program. Realistically, a certain amount of funds will be required to conduct a quality program. Yet, it should be pointed out that a large budget is not prerequisite to an efficient program. With wise planning and management much can be accom--plished even though large expenditures are not possible. However, if library orientation is included as one of the objectives of the library, then it is deserving of funds from the institutional budget, and fi--nancial support for the program should be assured through specific allotments in the library budget.

In addition to institutional funds there is the possibility of special grants, as has been the case for many of the good programs throughout the country. However, it must be pointed out that such funds are only temporary and that financial commitment on the part of the institution is important in order to sustain the program after the grant expires.

AUXILIARY PERSONNEL

Like the total library operation itself, much of the success of library orientation is dependent on many services and personnel who work behind the scenes. Scripts have to be written; slides, tapes and transparencies must be made; bibliographies must be prepared; along with innumerable jobs which require additional time and per--sonnel. The degree to which library orientation personnel have access to persons and facilities for accomplishing these types of jobs will do much to determine the extent and quality of the program. If the library is a media center, or if the audiovisual services are a part of the library, administratively, it probably will be easier to accom--plish some of these tasks. However, if not, then it will be necessary to make the proper contacts and arrangements for materials to be prepared elsewhere.

Library orientation personnel should have a large pool of people who can be called on for various kinds of assistance and services, ranging from the narration of scripts to art work in the preparation of materials, since most of the programs will have to be produced locally, due to the fact that few commercially prepared materials are available for college--level instruction, particularly those which can be used without some modification and/or adaptation. Although it is more desirable to have the various technical services, etc. available on campus for developing materials, library orientation personnel in colleges and universities not having extensive services should not overlook the possibility of talented members of the faculty and library staff who may volunteer services, or often student assistants can be very helpful under proper guidance.

SUMMARY AND CONCLUSIONS

What then should be the position of the orientation program within the library? It becomes readily apparent that no final answer could be given which would apply in all colleges and universities and to all programs. Just as in the total instructional program, there seems to be no standard practice which will be applicable to all institutions of higher education for library orientation and instruction. And although it is possible to develop objectives, principles, and other theoretical foundations on which a program should be based, it seems better to leave the techniques by which these will be accomplished to the judgment of the individuals who have the responsibility for planning to meet local needs. Therefore, from the influencing factors considered in the foregoing discussion, the following conclusions are given:

1. There is no common pattern regarding the administrative placement of the library orientation program.

2. Relatively few of the conference participants reported separate departments of library orientation.

3. One person should be given the responsibility for coordinating the library orientation program.

4. Regardless of the placement of the program, sufficient time should be specifically allotted to persons responsible for library orientation, and it should not be an added duty.

5. Financial support should be assured the library orientation program by specific allocations in the library budget if it is to be part of the total program.

6. If it is to be an important part of the total program, library orientation should be included in the stated objectives of the library and should be compatible with the overall objectives of the parent institution.

7. Where time, interest, expertise, and desire permit, the library staff should be shared on a cross-departmental basis in planning and conducting the library orientation program.

8. Among the colleges and universities represented at the conference there seemed to be no correlation between the size and type of institution and the type and quality of library orientation program.

9. Based on institutions represented at the conference, the

most common placement, administratively, of the library orientation program was the Public Services Area, most often as an auxiliary unit of the Reference Department.

10. The support and acceptance of the program by faculty, students, and college administration are crucial to the success of library orientation.

11. Library orientation is both needed and desired by graduate as well as undergraduate students.

12. Library orientation programs which are most likely to be successful over a long--range period are those which develop as a result of careful study and planning.

13. The understanding, acceptance, and assistance of other library personnel are important to the success of the library orientation program.

14. The administrative placement of the library orientation program is less important than the place it occupies in the collective thought of the academic community.

15. The position of the library orientation program, both administratively and otherwise, is influenced tremendously by the attitude of the director of the library and the active support which he or she gives it.

16. Library orientation is dependent on access to personnel and facilities for development of materials for use in the program.

17. The library orientation program will be more effective if all the personnel in the Public Services Area, including student assistants and paraprofessionals, are familiar with the program.

18. The persons who are given the responsibility for the library orientation program should be selected on the basis of qualifications, interest, and time available.

19. Libraries in which time, personnel, funds, and facilities are severely limited should not embark on an extensive program of library orientation initially, but should begin on a smaller scale and grow as these factors permit. Also, it is suggested that such libraries concentrate their efforts on methods which do not involve large amounts of time, money, and personnel in the early stages of their program (e.g., self--instruction, etc.).

In summary, it may be said that the instructional program of the library -- what is being placed, where it is placed, with whom and for whom it is placed, and how it is placed -- depends on many factors. Not the least of these is the perception of librarians of the most effective ways to fulfill the objective of developing the ability of library users to learn independently.

DOING IT:

THE METHODS AND MATERIALS OF INSTRUCTION

Robin Branstator

Discussion Leaders:
Sheila Berger Rice, University of Michigan
James Kennedy, Earlham College
Robin Branstator, Eastern Michigan University

The methods and materials of library instruction comprise such a vast area of thought that any one hour discussion of this multi-faceted subject will necessarily only scratch the surface. Each of the three discussion groups represented here approached the topic in different ways; each attempted in some way to confront the more problematic aspects of the topic. Major areas of concern to partici-pants were: the importance of overall program planning to devel-oping methods and materials, the effectiveness of audio--visual ma--terials, the motivation of students, and determining the amount of material to be presented to students.

It should be noted that one discussion group broke up into four "consciousness raising" groups to consider specific problems pro--posed by the discussion leader. The participants were encouraged to discuss as many forms of resolution to their problem as they could think of within the prescribed limits of preparation time, group size, finances, and so forth. They were asked to report on: 1) alternatives discussed; 2) the most agreeable solution; and 3) a description of what materials could be used most effectively. These problems and their suggested resolutions have been inserted into the following text.

PLANNING THE PROGRAM

Before embarking on the time–consuming and expensive planning prerequisite to creating appropriate methods and materials of library instruction, it is wise to review the goals of the library instruction program, whether proposed or already in existence. One premise is that program planning and materials are inextricably tied and that there is no single key to success in this area. Factors to consider are those that will contribute to a successful program. Some of these factors are: 1) the purpose or function of the pro--gram; 2) the characteristics of the group for which the program is being planned (size, level, background, etc.); 3) the amount of time and money available and, more importantly, the worth of the pro--

gram (i.e., money may be available, but only enough for a one–time program, and there is a limit as to how much that kind of program is worth); and 4) critical to the success of a program is the kind of talent or creative resources which are available.

This sounds like common sense, but in this age of A--V tech--nology we often lose sight of more creative and less expensive alter--natives. It is easy to turn to A--V technology and computers because the program, if it can be afforded, comes in such a neat package. By the same token, if the technology is available, it should be the pro--gram planner's responsibility to maximize its potential use.

Failures of library instruction programs must be continually taken into account in order to spot methods and materials which may need to be revised or discarded. As one discussion leader noted, "Yogi Berra said, 'You can observe a lot just by watching.' " Aware--ness of the library instruction programs of other institutions and communication between such institutions is essential to the vitality and effectiveness of methods and materials. Exchange of ideas and of physical materials themselves is a most desirable interaction.

INSTRUCTIONAL MATERIALS

Instructional materials may be considered in terms of form. The forms are fairly well known to all librarians involved in library instruction. There are transparencies, slides, records, films, tapes, duplicated materials, posters, photographs, pictures, maps, graphs, charts, games, videotape, and other more sophisticated electronic media.

Of these, the use of A--V materials was of great interest to the conference participants. It was generally agreed that many students resist utilizing such materials. In addition, many A--V materials were considered to be irrelevant to immediate instructional needs. On the other hand, although the physical presence of the librarian was felt to be desirable, A--V materials were deemed necessary when the li--brary instruction program is faced with the task of reaching large numbers of students. Several participants expressed the fear that, while A--V materials may communicate information to large numbers of students, that fact often leads library instruction librarians to re--lax, feeling they have done their job. The overwhelming consensus was that merely *reaching* students is not enough; they should also learn some basic library skills.

Most participants felt that A–V materials have their place with--in the instructional program if only to orient students to the physical aspects of the library and to general research tools. However, when library instruction is to be applied to upper level students, the small group or librarian--led siminar approach is preferred. The point was made that library instruction is supposed to enable students to do independent research and not to depend on methods such as an A--V presentation to prepare and digest information for them.

The realization that today's students are, as members of a tele-vision culture, visually oriented must influence the choice of library instruction materials selected for use. A--V materials can, therefore, be effectively used to convey information, provided, of course, that the materials are well done. The student's ability to make the tran-sition from A--V materials to print reference works, for example, was considered to be a major problem.

The quality of currently available A--V materials was the subject of some concern. Admitting that most students today are visually oriented implies that they are more acutely aware of good visual techniques and therefore will be quickly "turned off" by poorly done video or slide--tape productions, for instance. It was highly recommended that before creating any type of A--V presentation, appropriate A--V experts be consulted.

Some students will, it was felt, resist this approach and not derive as much information from A--V materials as from other sources. They are still oriented to the traditional lecture and depend on print resources for information. The A--V program, however, can be an effective supplement to the lecture, particularly as an aid in reviewing areas still unclear after the lecture.

Some participants wondered if the sole use of A--V materials would reach the student who would not normally approach a librar-ian for assistance or who would not even use the library at all. It was felt that the student who would not admit his or her ignorance to a person might feel less reluctant to do so in front of a computer or slide projector. However, A--V materials were considered inadequate in that they so often do not answer the specific question the student has in mind. The student may therefore feel that his or her time has been wasted on a program providing only general information.

Consciousness Raising Problem -- One

Two thousand freshmen are enrolled for the fall term and are supposed to come to your library for orientation one day during registration. They expect to get a sense of your library, i.e., where things are, how to get around, how to check out a book, and so forth. The program should be short and to the point. Since it is the beginning of the term, most of the library staff is going to be very busy, but one or two other librarians have volunteered to help you out. Fortunately, you have all summer to work on the program, and because so many people are involved, you need to start planning early. You not only need to work out the program, but you must also devise ways to promote it. The library has agreed that a small amount of money ($40.00) may be used for materials. Outline a program and the way you would promote it. You may schedule the time(s) for the program.

* * * * * * *

After considering several alternative types of tour, including lining up staff members to take groups through the library on a regular schedule every fifteen minutes or so, the group finally decided that some sort of A--V presentation would be most suitable for a group of this size. Within the budget limitations however, no one was very happy with any of the alternatives mentioned.

Consideration was also given to the areas of library orientation and instruction to which the various forms of materials may be applied. These areas include such projects as programmed teaching aids, guides of various sorts, tours, lectures, seminars, and class situations. There are other applications to be sure. Using the ex-- ample of a self--guided tour suggests several possibilities. A self-- guided tour may require portable tape cassette players, maps, or written sets of instructions, to name a few. Which of these forms to use will be determined largely by the factors mentioned previously (i.e., money available, time, size of the group, etc.) and the physical layout of the library.

INSTRUCTIONAL METHODS

Regarding methods of library instruction, several problems were discussed, with primary focus on the motivation of students and de-- termining the proper amount of material to present to them.

Methods for teaching search strategy occupied the discussion of one group which felt that such instruction involves the presentation of two basic concepts: 1) the concept of the ideal bibliography in which the student's library search is virtually completed if he or she can find a recent, authoritative, annotated bibliography which cites books and articles on the topic; and 2) the concept of beginning broadly on a topic and gradually narrowing it to manageable limits. This concept involves beginning with summary articles in encyclo-- pedias or textbooks and then proceeding to bibliographies, indexes, and like tools to find materials on the topic.

Motivation

How does one get the student to see the need for instruction in the use of the library? This query prompted numerous responses, which varied according to the type of library instruction program in operation and on the type of student under consideration. Gener--ally agreed upon was the basic premise that all tools, facilities and resources are inextricably tied to bibliographic research. Some participants stressed the need for assignment related instruction, preferably that requiring a bibliography. However, there will still be students who feel they know all there is to know about using the library, but by relating specific research tools to a student's topic, this resistance to instruction can often be overcome.

Several library instruction librarians working with introductory classes favored the method of requiring that a library assignment be done prior to the formal library lecture. This method appears to force the student to recognize his or her limitations, particularly if he or she is forbidden to solicit help from the reference desk. For example, the assignment might present the student with a series of questions pertaining to a specific topic, such as: 1) Which encyclopedia, other than the general adult encyclopedias, will give you a good introduction to your topic? 2) What are the titles of several dictionaries that would be useful in defining terms related to your topic? 4) What are the proper headings under which to look for your topic? In this case the resulting papers are not collected, but are checked to ascertain whether or not they have been completed, so the student's degree of ignorance is revealed only to him or her--self.

Many participants felt that students will often listen more read--ily to one another than to a librarian and that the wise librarian will exploit this tendency. For example, in a lecture or group situation the librarian might ask if any of the students know how the subject headings work and allow the person who responds to explain the process, being ready to supply other information as needed.

It was stressed that vital to motivating students is the avoidance of technical library jargon. Many library terms will simply not be intelligible to students, especially undergraduates. It is necessary to continually gauge the comprehension of the audience and to be able to explain and describe research tools and methods concisely. It is also necessary to be aware of current student interests, so that in the preparation and presentation of materials, the librarian can relate library research to these interests.

Consciousness Raising Problem -- Two

You read in the student newspaper that the results of a survey of freshman in the college for which you are the orientation--instruc--tion librarian indicate that about one hundred students will need to improve basic skills in order to survive academically. These students come from particularly poor areas where quality secondary educa--

tion does not exist. In order to facilitate learning for these students, the college has decided to create four English classes that will concentrate on developing skills -- reading skills, writing skills, note--taking skills, etc. You decide that it would be appropriate to suggest that library skills also be included. Since these students will be sensitive about being singled out, it is important to develop a program in which there will be good reinforcement for learning. What kind of program would you develop?

* * * * * * *

The group agreed that the best solution would be to team teach the English skills classes if possible. An important criterion in teaching such a group is that materials relate to interesting subjects. Also discussed was the possibility of having an area where materials for these students would be set aside. Bibliographies on subjects of interest were also suggested. Another idea was the possibility of training some students to help these "skills" students as students might better relate to each other than to a librarian. A final consideration was for materials of the self--directed type. All these ideas seemed likely possibilities.

Consciousness Raising Problem -- Three

An instructor of an introductory psychology course has asked you to discuss library materials relating to psychology with her class. She has stated, however, that she does not believe in the grade as "carrot" and feels that an out--of--class assignment or paper should not be necessary to reinforce your presentation. She believes that the class will be interested because the discussion will be valuable to them. You, on the other hand, are skeptical about the potential for enthusiasm among the group. You know that many of these students are only taking this class to fill a requirement; yet, you hate to lose an opportunity for helping students learn about library materials. How do you think you can best deal with this situation?

* * * * * * *

This problem stymied the group and only one major point came out of the discussion. The point was that, given the instructor's posture, the librarian would have to work around an interesting and/or popular topic in order to keep the students' attention.

Amount of Material to Present

How much material is too much is a question which concerns many library instruction librarians and it appeared frequently in the discussions. Will you destroy the delicate achievement of having reached a student by overwhelming the motivated or partially motivated student with masses of facts, or masses of duplicated pages, study guides, bibliographies, and so forth? The responses to this problem were varied, depending on the type of student to be instructed.

It is important to first accurately determine the level of the student to be instructed, to put oneself in his or her position. If the student is completely unfamiliar with the *Readers' Guide,* for example, a copy of a sample page may be very helpful. Or if working on a particular topic, the student will often appreciate a brief study guide or bibliography indicating especially useful resources.

It was generally agreed that presenting or handing out too few materials is preferable to doing the opposite which all too often results in wastebaskets bulging with discarded, unread handouts or in minds which have absorbed nothing of what was presented. It is most important to present the student with enough information to recognize the existence and basic purpose of a reference tool or research method. Armed with this knowledge, the student can then solicit more information when he or she feels the need for it.

CONCLUSION

The final consciousness raising problem deals with a situation all too familiar to library instruction librarians. It covers a wide range of problems involved in developing effective methods and materials.

Consciousness Raising Problem -- Four

A sociology professor has assigned his introductory, independent study class of three hundred students a workbook to complete. One of the exercises relates specifically to library materials. The exercise requires students to find statistical materials about subjects related to sociology and their specialized tools. However the students have little sense of how or where to look up such things. They do not know, for instance, that in order to find information about world population it is necessary to find the subject heading *Population -- Statistics.* Nor do United Nations sources pop into their heads. The professor feels it is important for the students to learn to use the library and not to ask the reference librarian for answers. Unfortunately, you have only just learned about this exercise incidentally from a member of the class who wanted to start early. Most of the class will be in the library in the next two weeks. Because it is an independent study group, there are no class meetings. How would you propose to help these students?

* * * * * * *

There are two points on which the group agreed immediately. The first was that a librarian would have to contact the professor, and the second was that whatever the library chose to do, it would probably not be done too well the first time. Hopefully, by contacting the professor, it would not be the same kind of problem if the situation arose again. In the meantime, it seemed reasonable to prepare a brief "pathfinder" or guide for the students currently working on their library exercise. A display in a prominent place in the library would also provide a series of helpful hints.

The group also engaged in a discussion of whether or not the library should do anything at all. Some group members assumed the professor just did not realize the difficulty the students would have with this exercise. Others thought the professor fully intended for the students to work entirely on their own. At any rate, all agreed communication with the professor was the most critical issue.

It is apparent from the preceding pages that many librarians are still in a quandary as to the best methods and materials for sound instruction in library use. There appears to be no set formula for developing the most creative and effective ways of achieving such instruction. Conference participants agreed that if the high standards of a good library instruction program are to be met, the librarian must evince a genuine concern for the student and relate directly to his or her needs. In addition, the librarian must maintain flexibility and openmindness regarding the development of both methods and materials.

EVALUATION OF LIBRARY ORIENTATION AND INSTRUCTION PROGRAMS:

A TAXONOMY

Thomas Kirk

Discussion Leaders:
James Doyle, University of Detroit
Mary Jo Lynch, University of Michigan
Thomas Kirk, Earlham College

The final discussion topic was the evaluation of library orien-- tation and instruction programs. Because there has been so little evaluation of library instruction and because so many people pre-- sent at the conference were searching for information rather than offering to contribute, the discussions did not explore topics in any depth. The discussions tended to be a series of monologues with little give and take or questioning by the participants.

Because of the nature of these discussions, the best way to summarize and present a coherent picture of what happened is to present in outline form (with comment) a number of the major points about the evaluation of library instruction. As the material from the discussions was assembled it became clear that the major thrust of the discussions centered around the listing, describing, and differentiating of the various types of evaluation, the several purposes for which evaluation might be carried out, and the prob-- lems which are associated with getting significant evaluation. There-- fore, the proceedings of the three discussions on evaluation are out-- lined along these lines:

I. Informal evaluation
    1. Personal radar
    2. See--how--they--run
    3. Brief questionnaires
    4. Casual observation
II. Formal Evaluation
    1. Content
       a. Standardized tests
       b. Home--made tests
    2. Product
       a. Paper grades
       b. Bibliography evaluation
    3. Process
       a. Journals/Diaries

b. Work sheets (Pathfinders)
  4. Attitudes
  5. Cost--effectiveness
III. Objectives
IV. Other considerations

I. INFORMAL EVALUATION

The participants found it useful to distinguish informal from formal evaluation. Informal evaluation includes a number of subjective measures which the librarian can use to assess student progress within a particular library instruction activity. The main emphasis of this type of evaluation is to get a sense of what is going on in as quick and simple a manner as possible. What things did students like or dislike about the instruction? What problems do they still have? How should the instruction be changed the next time? Etc. In other words, "the librarian is getting feedback" from the students, faculty, and other librarians.

One of the major conclusions of the discussion about the importance of this form of evaluation was that reference librarians should be involved in the instructional program. Their involvement, it was concluded, would help the feedback process and therefore make it more likely that the instruction would improve.

This form of evaluation is not very precise and is therefore not intended to give precise measurements of how much students learned. Nor could these types of evaluation be used to make any definitive statements comparing one form or type of instruction with another.

The forms of informal evaluation that were identified include:
1. *Personal radar.*

The librarian is watching for clues to the students' attitude toward the instruction: facial expressions, attention, is the student grasping what is being given, do the students ask intelligent questions, do they ask for more information. It was pointed out that this form of evaluation is perhaps *the* major way in which faculty assess their successes and failures.
2. *See--how--they--run.*

This consists of routine observation of how students handle things when they are in the library. Can students make use of the sources about which they have been told?
3. *The quickie questionnaire.*

This is not a formal carefully designed questionnaire but simply a few direct questions for which the librarian wants some student response which will indicate students' reaction to the instruction: Did the students like it? Did they learn anything? How should it be changed?

4. *Casual conversation.*

This is a more pointed way of getting selected feedback from faculty, students, and other librarians. However, direct comments to librarians on their instruction are not likely to be negative. Generally the negative feedback from conversation will be more indirect: A faculty member or librarian mentioning the difficulty which they observed students having, or reports from some students on how other students responded to the instruction.

II. FORMAL EVALUATION

Formal evaluation consists of structured and systematic mech-- anisms for collecting information about an instructional program. The reasons for such an evaluation are many: To compare one pro-- gram with another; to measure the success of a program; or to dem- onstrate the educational value of a program. In formal evaluation much more care must be given to the details of evaluation design and the conclusions which the results can support. These considerations are important because while the individual librarian providing the in- struction may be interested, the results and the supported conclu- sions are generally for someone else's benefit. Usually the results must satisfactorily convince outsiders of the conclusions the librarian draws.

1. *Content.*

The evaluation of library instruction may focus on several dif-- ferent aspects. Here the concern is for how much of the specific con- tent of the instructional package has been mastered by the students. This focus usually concerns itself with the hows of using specific li- brary materials and reference tools, procedures for using the library, and other specific knowledge which the instructional program has tried to convey to the student because of a belief that command of that information is essential to effective use of the library. This form of evaluation has been most frequently used in the past and has generally taken one of two forms: a. *Standardized tests,* and b. *Home--made tests.*

a. *Standardized tests.* There really has been only one standardized test which has received wide usage, the Columbia University's *A Li- brary Orientation Test for College Freshmen.* However, the test covers only the very basic concepts involved in library usage and therefore has little value in assessing the students' comprehension of material covered in a particular instructional or orientation program. Because of the lack of any satisfactory standardized test which will evaluate detailed and sophisticated aspects of library usage, there is considerable interest in the development of such an instrument.

b. *Home–made tests.* The absence of any satisfactory standardized test has resulted in the development of a great many different tests for each evaluation program. Most of the local tests developed to date have been used as screening devices to ascertain the level of competence of entering students. In a few cases (Wiggins, 1972; Kirk, 1971) local tests were developed to evaluate success in the content retention of students participating in a particular instruc-- tional program.

These tests however, do not serve the profession very well. They frequently are not well constructed, and they have not been used with a large enough group of subjects to establish reliable means. Furthermore, there is not general agreement within the pro- fession about the general appropriateness of the test items.

Of course the development of reliable validated tests is a dif-- ficult and time--consuming task. Librarians who are considering the development of such a test for local use should study carefully the work that has previously been done, study the literature of test de-- velopment (e.g. Kemp, 1971), and consult some of the expertise that is available on their own campus.

2. *Product.*

There is considerable dissatisfaction with content testing be-- cause it does not provide a valid measure of whether a student can use the library. In place of this form of testing librarians have turned their attention to the assessment of the products of student library use.

a. *Paper grades.* In this case librarians are asking faculty to look at the students' work and make some judgement as to whether library instruction has helped improve the quality of the assignments. The immediate difficulty is that of ascertaining what the faculty evaluates when they grade papers. If the faculty are only interested in the students' ability to construct a well expressed and logical argument for the points being made, then library use is not likely to have an effect which changes in grade can demonstrate. On the other hand, if faculty do evaluate sources of information and the use of sources to develop and defend a thesis, then changes in grades are more likely to be attributable to library instruction.

In any case, correlation studies of students' grades on papers resulting from library use and library instruction seem, at best, to be an indirect way of getting at the real question: Can the student pro– duce a better bibliography as a result of library instruction? This is not to argue, however, that this type of correlation study is not valuable. If the intent is to try to convince faculty that library in-- struction will help students do better work for the faculty member, then this type of study seems ideal.

b. *Bibliography evaluation.* In this case an attempt is made to assess the quality of the bibliography which a student has collected. In order to do a systematic study, bibliographies prepared by the students before and after library instruction have to be collected and evaluated and the results compared, or matched groups, some re--ceiving and others not receiving instruction, have to be compared.

The problem with such an evaluation is the difficulty in getting workable criteria for evaluating the bibliography. If the evaluation has to be done by a subject specialist who reviews the bibliography to see that all "essential" items are included, that citations repre--senting the major schools of thought are present, and that the cita--tions are the most relevant to the topic of the paper, then consider--able time will have to be invested. More time than it is probably realistic to expect can be provided for such an effort. On the other hand, if there are certain criteria which indirectly measure the quality of a bibliography and which can be applied by someone who is only moderately informed about the subject matter of a field, then per--haps a less time consuming, more objective form of evaluation can be accomplished.

The only use of bibliography evaluation in formal research was that of Kirk (1971). However, the criteria used were vague and thus required considerable subjective evaluation on the part of the inves--tigator. Since that study, the criteria have been revised with the in--tent of making it possible to apply them on a more objective basis. The present edition looks something like this:

Criteria	*Score*
1. The appropriateness of the material cited as sources of information for a scholarly paper in biology. (Appropriateness *equals* reputation of source, age of source, etc.)	5 4 3 2 1 0
2. The appropriateness of the material cited as sources of information for the particular subject being studied. (Appropriateness *e--quals* reputation of source, age, author authority)	5 4 3 2 1 0
3. A reasonable number of primary sources, from a variety of titles. This shows some confrontation with the indexing services that are available. (1 point/source)	5 4 3 2 1 0
4. Inclusion of the several most important secondary sources and texts in the field being studied. (2 points/source)	5 4 3 2 1 0

45

5. Number of references. Anything less than   3 2 1 0
   10 items would raise the question of com--
   pleteness. This will vary greatly from sub--
   ject to subject and must be considered a
   minor point.   (less than 4 sources -- 0
   points; 4--6 sources -- 1 pt.; 7--9 sources --
   2 pts.; 10 or more sources -- 3 pts.)

6. Consistent acceptable format used in the   3 2 1 0
   cited literature section. (Inconsistent for--
   mat, incomplete information -- 0 pts.; in--
   consistent format, complete information --
   1 pt.; acceptable, consistent format with
   complete information -- 3 pts.)

Bibliography evaluation can and is being used in a number of different ways as a regular part of an instructional program. In this way it serves both as a feedback mechanism and as a technique for the overall evaluation of a program. In these programs students are required, at some point preliminary to the completion of the assign--ment, to turn in a bibliography for their topic. The bibliography is then critiqued by the librarian and returned with comments and suggestions or additional search strategies.

3. *Process.*

While the evaluation of product does address itself more di--rectly to the question of how well students can use the library there remains one more aspect that can be added, the process. The pro--duct of any library use can be obtained in a number of different ways. Library instruction hopefully will help students learn the most efficient techniques for use of the library. It is these tech--niques of process by which students gather library information that must be evaluated as well as the end product itself.

Patricia Knapp in the *Monteith College Library Experiment* (1967) first suggests this possibility. She also relates how difficult it is to collect valid reliable data on the students' process of collecting library information.

a. *Journals or diaries.* Journals and diaries offer one possible way of collecting information on how the student actually used the li--brary. With the cooperation of faculty, the librarian asks the stu--dents to write down, as they do their library search, what they actually did: What reference tools they used; the order in which they used them; what they expected to find; what they actually found. The librarian can then look at the journals to see what kinds of things students are doing in their use of the library.

There are several difficulties that must be overcome if the jour--

nal method is to be used effectively. The librarian must have approval from the faculty to do it and some way of motivating students to write the journal. Once the climate is set so that students and faculty take the assignment seriously, the librarian must be concerned with the kind of information the student puts down. Ideally the student should be able to discriminate between the important information and the trivial. Unfortunately this is not the case, so that if a student is asked to write all the things he or she did in the library which were involved in the search, the journals will come back with different types of information from different students. It is therefore very difficult to compare journals or synthesize the result into any conclusion. To overcome this difficulty, a form can be developed which suggests or directs what information is to be supplied. This kind of assignment is more of a worksheet of "Pathfinder" (Stevens, 1973).

b. *Worksheets and "Pathfinders"*. In this situation, instead of asking the student to write down everything that he or she did in the process of using the library, the student is given a worksheet. The worksheet begins by asking for the topic on which the student is working. Then the student is asked to list by reference book category (dictionaries, encyclopedias, handbooks, bibliographies, indexes) the actual titles used. The worksheets would list the categories that are appropriate for the particular assignment. These types of work --sheets can be used both as an evaluation device and as a feedback mechanism to help the librarian diagnose students' problems and help them. After a student has completed a worksheet there might be some follow--up with an interview or lecture.

The worksheet might be further structured so that the entire search is laid out for the student. Therefore, when the student completes the assignment he has essentially produced his own "Pathfinder." In this form the librarian can fairly easily determine whether the student has made an efficient search.

4. *Attitudes.*

While it is important to know just how much students got out of an instruction program and to what degree the students' behavior has been changed as a result of the program, it is also important to know what students' attitudes are towards the library and how they were changed by library instruction. The library instruction and o--rientation program must change the attitudes of library users into positive relationships or positive feelings towards the library and librarians. This kind of attitude will result in greater use of the library, not just for the required things, but whenever information is desired -- while the student is in college and long afterwards.

5. *Cost--effectiveness.*

Another type of measurement is efficiency -- in other words, cost. Many libraries are within the constraints of program budgeting now and efficiency is just another way of saying cost effectiveness. How much does an instruction or orientation program cost per learner? If you are operating a small program it doesn't seem as important, but even when the expenditure is minor, if you can supply the library director or budget controller with sound information on the cost effectiveness of a program, it is going to impress him or her.

Here is a simple formula. Development cost is basically staff time. How many hours were spent developing the program and how much was the hourly rate? In addition, who produces the materials and how much do they get paid per hour? And who took the pictures and how much are they paid per hour? You add all this up to get a development cost. Then add that to equipment cost plus the supply and materials cost. Then divide the total by the number of learners who are above an acceptable level of success. The failures cannot be counted here. The figure is the cost per learner.

DEVELOPMENT COST (Staff Time)

+ Equipment Cost
+ Supplies and Materials
÷ Number of Successful Learners

= Cost Per Learner

This implies that if you are attempting to train 1,000 students and only 10 of them succeed, your cost per learner is going to be sky high. With the cost effectiveness approach there has to be a level below which you have a failure and above which there is success.

III. OBJECTIVES

Evaluation of a program will indicate the purposes or objectives of an instructional program. If the evaluation procedure is not to dictate the objectives, the objectives should be carefully thought out prior to the implementation of the program. Evaluation techniques which will check for the achievement of those objectives can then be developed.

An important aspect of new ideas about instruction is that objectives should be articulated in terms of the behavior which one expects from students as a result of the instruction. Evaluation of the program then should measure to what extent the students' behavior is like the behavior the program is intended to produce.

The development of such objectives is an extremely difficult and time consuming activity and requires a certain amount of expertise. Therefore it would be useful to practicing librarians if some professional group, such as a committee in ALA or ACRL, would develop such objectives and develop a mechanism for evaluating the success of a program based on those objectives.[1]

IV. OTHER CONSIDERATIONS

The taxonomy presented does describe and contrast the various techniques of evaluation that were discussed by the Evaluation Discussion Groups at the Conference. But there were also a number of additional issues and problems that do not relate solely to one or another of the evaluation techniques but are relevant to the entire consideration of evaluation. What follows is a capsulized description of these basic considerations.

1. *Evaluation in a program vs. evaluation of a program.*

Several times in the earlier portions of this presentation mention was made of the possible use of evaluation techniques in the actual instruction program to facilitate feedback and help the learning process. This is generally true of almost all evaluation procedures. However, there are likely to be differences between evaluation procedures that assist the student and librarian in understanding the students' problems, and those procedures which are used to determine whether the program achieves its objectives.

2. *Evaluation of the achievement of long and short term objectives.*

There are usually some specific short term objectives which an instructional program tries to achieve and some long term effects which it is hoped will permanently change the students' outlook and attitude toward libraries. Most evaluation, what little has been done so far, has focused only on the question of short term objectives. As more and more students pass through a library orientation or instruction program, there should be some kind of study which looks at some of the more general aspects of citizen attitude toward, and use of, libraries and whether there is any correlation with the various types and/or amount of library instruction they had while in school.

3. *Literature on the subject.*

If one searches the literature on the topic of instruction in the use of the library one is apt to think in terms of searching *Library Literature, Education Index,* and *Research in Education* under the topic of library instruction. In doing the search three different terms might be emphasized: LIBRARY instruction; instruction in USE of the library; or library INSTRUCTION. In *Library Literature* and the education indexes the first two emphases do not give good results. However, if a search is made looking for material on instruction, instructional design, objectives writing, and other related aspects, one will find a tremendous number of relevant citations. This is just one aspect of the overall tendency of librarians to dissassociate their problems in providing and evaluating library instruction from the general field of education and educational research. Just as librarians expect others to come to libraries for information and expertise on information organization, so librarians should turn to the expertise which the education community can offer in solving our instruction-al problems.

4. *Library instruction and reference services.*

There have been conflicting comments on the effect of library instruction on reference services. Some have claimed that with library instruction there will be less need for students to ask the reference staff for help. This line of reasoning would lead one to conclude that if the number of reference questions declines then the library instruction program has been effective. However, others (Wilkinson, 1972) have shown that with an extensive instruction program the number of questions is larger. Therefore, the same results might be interpreted exactly the opposite. The profession needs more information on the effect of library instruction on the number and type of reference questions before the data can be used to conclude anything about the success or failure of an instruction program.

FOOTNOTES

[1]Editor's note: The ACRL Bibliographic Instruction Task Force is working on just such objectives. Copies of the objectives are available from the Task Force.

BIBLIOGRAPHY

Kemp, J. (1971) *Instructional Design, a Plan for Unit and Course Development.* Belmont, Calif., Fearon, 122pp.

Kirk, Thomas G. (1971) "Comparison of Two Methods of Library Instruction for Students in Introductory Biology," *College and Research Libraries,* 32(6): 465--474.

Knapp, Patricia (1966) *The Monteith College Library Experiment.* New York, Scarecrow Press, 293pp.

Stevens, Charles H. (1972) "Library Pathfinders: A New Possibility for Cooperative Reference Service," *College and Research Li-raries,* 34(1): 40--46.

Wiggins, Marvin E. and D. Stewart Low (1972) "Use of an Instruc—

tion Psychology Model for Development of Library–Use Instructional Programs," *Drexel Library Quarterly,* 8(3): 269-
280.

Wilkinson, Billy R. (1972) *Reference Service for Undergraduate Students; Four Case Studies.* Metuchen, N.J., Scarecrow Press, 421pp.

PROJECT LOEX: THE FIRST YEAR

Mary Bolner
Eastern Michigan University

Library orientation--instruction is currently one of the in things in the academic world. The past few years have seen a tremendous increase in the number of publications, committees, conferences and workshops dealing with the subject.

The concept of Project LOEX grew out of one of these con-- ferences: the First Annual Conference on Library Orientation for Academic Libraries, held at Eastern Michigan University in May, 1971. The Project itself was formally established one year later at the Second Annual Conference. At that time the Project's objectives were outlined and discussion centered around what LOEX would be. Now at the Third Annual Conference, we can report what the Project has become and discuss what it may yet become in the future.

The acronym "LOEX" stands for Library Orientation Ex– change, with "orientation" referring to all forms of instruction in library use. That includes everything from the basic tour covering the library's physical lay--out, to advanced bibliographic instruction for graduate students and faculty. The Project's major objective is to facilitate communication among academic libraries with orientation and instruction programs, to assist academic libraries interested in developing such programs, and to aid individual librarians and library science educators and students in their research endeavors. In meeting this goal, it functions as a cooperative clearinghouse for orientation and instruction information and materials. Each member library deposits information and materials relating to its own pro– gram and, in exchange, has access to the data deposited by all other members.

The first year of the Project's existence has been primarily one of getting started, of finding out what's going on and developing ways to let people know about it. Members have been solicited, in– formation and materials have been collected and organized for re-- trieval, and information has been disseminated. By January, 1973, the Project consisted of 100 member libraries and had become an operational clearinghouse, disseminating information on request. In the five months since then, 20 requests for information on various methods of instruction and types of materials have been filled, most of them by referral to other members who have supplied the actual *how--to--do--it* information. In addition, the first issue of the *LOEX News,* a periodical newsletter, was published in mid--March.

Today (May 4, 1973), 139 academic libraries are members of Project LOEX. They represent 40 states, Washington, D.C., Puerto Rico, and 4 Canadian provinces. Among the members are 31 two--year junior or community college libraries (22 percent), 29 under--graduate libraries (21 percent), 64 combination undergraduate--graduate libraries (46 percent), 9 graduate libraries (7 percent), and 6 subject or divisional libraries within a system (4 percent). The enrollment served ranges from 200 students for a graduate divisional library to 41,000 for a combination undergraduate--graduate library.

The orientation and instruction programs of the Project's members can be summarized as follows:

Staffing patterns: The programs of 126 members (91 percent) are conducted by reference and/or subject librarians on a part--time basis. Only 3 members (2 percent) have full--time positions, and 10 (7 percent) have both full and part--time positions. In the latter case, the part--time people are generally subject librarians who provide instruction in their areas of responsibility.

Patrons provided orientation--instruction: As would be expected, the type of library determines to a great extent the type of patron provided the service, i.e., two--year college libraries emphasize primarily the freshman and, secondarily, the sophomore levels, and libraries serving graduate and professional enrollments provide service primarily for graduate students. Those libraries serving either undergraduates only, or both undergraduates and graduates, emphasize the first two levels with gradually decreasing coverage for juniors, seniors and graduates. Faculty members at 49 (35 percent) of the institutions are also offered orientation and/or instruction.

Subject areas covered: Members provide instruction in thirty--six subject areas in addition to basic library use. Heaviest emphasis is placed on English, with slightly lesser coverage of the social and behavioral sciences, business, biology, chemistry, art, education, music and speech. Instruction in any area will be provided on request by 49 (35 percent) members.

Methods utilized: All members employ a combination of methods rather than relying on just one. The theory seems to be that each method (or type of material) works to some extent in a particular situation and that ideally all possibilities should be covered.

The most popular method of orientation is the conducted tour, offered by 105 members (76 percent). Other types of tour utilized are: printed guided by 26 members (19 percent); cassette guided by 15 members (11 percent); and slide--tape by 12 members (9 percent). Two types of tour are provided by 24 members (17 percent) and 3 types are offered by 4 members (3 percent).

The most widely employed instructional method is the class lecture, offered by 102 members (73 percent). The lecture may be general or subject--specific, may be held in the library or classroom, and may or may not be accompanied by an assignment or exercise.

Next in frequency of use is individual instruction, reported by 86 members (62 percent). This figure is probably misleading, however, as the question did not distinguish between individual instruction and the normally provided reference assistance.

The third most frequently employed method of instruction is the separate course in general library use or bibliography, which is reported by 30 members (22 percent).

Other instructional methods reported as being in use include consultation with faculty members, independent study programs, and term paper clinics.

Materials utilized: Print: As they do with methods, members utilize instructional materials in combination, with print materials much more heavily employed than non--print items. Of print materials, subject bibliographies are most frequently used, as reported by 90 members (65 percent), and subject guides (how to find information on a specific subject) are used by 51 members (37 percent).

The library handbook is another very popular form of instructional aid. Student handbooks are used by 84 members (60 percent) and faculty handbooks by 31 members (23 percent).

Assignments or exercises used alone or in connection with a class lecture or tour are used by 49 members (35 percent) and programmed instruction by 19 (14 percent). Textbooks and/or manuals are generally used in the separate courses offered by 30 members (22 percent).

Materials utilized: Non--print: As mentioned earlier, non--print items are much less used than print. This may be due to the expense involved and the expertise required to produce them. No form of non--print instructional material is used by 32 members (23 percent).

The slide--tape presentation is the most frequently used form, being reported by 47 members (34 percent). Such presentations, which appear to be quite popular with students, are generally used for orientation "tours", and instruction in the use of the card catalog and indexes. Slides and tapes (or cassettes) are also used separately

by 27 members (20 percent) and 33 members (24 percent), respec--
tively.

Transparencies are employed in class lectures and the separate
courses by 21 members (15 percent). Other forms of non--print
materials include: films, used by 8 members (6 percent); filmstrips,
used by 15 members (11 percent); television and/or videotape, also
used by 15 members (11 percent); and computers, used by 6 mem--
bers (4 percent).

Publicity: Personal contact with faculty members is definitely
the most frequently used method of publicizing the program, being
used by 112 members (80 percent). Personal contact with students,
used by 78 members (56 percent), also appears to be an effective
means of publicity. Other methods include: announcements and
advertisements in student publications, used by 57 members (41
percent); signs, posters, bulletin boards, used by 13 members (9
percent); and library publications, used by 5 members (4 percent).

Evaluation of the program: The development of valid methods
of evaluating our orientation and instruction efforts poses a
monumental problem for most of us. We know it is an essential
part of developing and maintaining a viable program. Yet
too many of us tend to ignore it, hoping it will go away, or we go at
it in a superficial manner out of ignorance, when all around us is the
expertise we need. Our colleagues in the sociology, psychology and
education departments are an all too often untapped source of assis--
tance.

Only 97 members (60 percent) report attempts at evaluation.
Of these, only 2 (1 percent) utilize control and experimental groups.
Other methods employed include: written evaluation by students
(generally in the form of a questionnaire), by 31 members (22 per--
cent); tests and/or exercises, by 24 members (17 percent); informal
observations of student performance, by 7 members (5 percent); in--
formal discussion with faculty members, by 20 members (14 per--
cent); and informal discussion with students, by 16 members (12
percent). The last method is generally used in combination with an--
other one.

Research in progress: Twenty--seven librarians participating in
the Project report research activities. Representative of these activi--
ties are surveys of existing programs, comparison of the effectiveness
of various instructional methods and materials, the utilization of
behavior modification principles in instruction, and the utilization of
control and experimental groups in evaluation.

In conclusion, it is obvious that there is really no such thing as
a "typical" program. Each is, to a certain extent, unique, being
shaped by local demands and resources. What is typical, however, is
the concern with quality orientation and instruction of the librarians

involved as demonstrated by their participation in Project LOEX.

Because of this concern and the willingness of people to share their own experiences with their colleagues, the future of the Project appears to be a bright one, filled with opportunities to serve the pro-- fession and to share in the development of an important and exciting field. Projections for the Project's second year include an increased membership accompanied by an increase in the number of requests for information and expansion of the *LOEX News* and other services. In relation to this latter area, suggestions are welcome and, in fact, requested. Through communication and cooperation we can pro-- gress toward our common goal.

ORIENTATION FOR WHAT?

Albert P. Marshall
Eastern Michigan University

There are a few basic assumptions which we might say are being used to carve out a special kind of library service, currently called Orientation. But fundamental to this service must be an under-- standing of libraries and what they generally try to do for the indi- vidual; and second, there must be a sincere love and respect for people as human beings. Once we have those, we merely have to put together a number of basic beliefs in order to arrive at Library Orientation. These may be listed as follows:

1. People respond to sincere offers of help, especially when they recognize their need for it.

2. People in general can recognize insincerity in others, just as a child can read emotional changes in the faces of its parents.

3. It is impossible for everybody to know everything, but librar-- ians do develop a particular expertise for ferreting out bits of infor- mation which help patrons to put together the core of an idea, to develop a thesis, to fill in the parts of a larger idea just as one might locate a lost part of a jigsaw puzzle.

4. Learning comes from every kind of experience, but basically our vocation is to provide the proper materials when the patron needs them.

5. Books are basic to learning. Through them we can help patrons develop their knowledge. All of the great ideas which man has de- veloped can be transmitted in a manner which hopefully awakens a spark which, in turn, helps to produce other great ideas for the good of mankind.

6. People can be helped to overcome their fear of libraries. When they begin to understand basically what libraries are all about, how to properly use the tools of the library, and that librarians are human resources which can be tapped for a special kind of help, patrons are likely to develop habits of good library usage.

7. Students who develop good library habits early are more likely to be better contributors than those who do not.

8. Teaching faculty members are not always good library users,

but they have a tremendous influence upon how their students de-- velop as library users.

9. Providing teachers with information widens their own know-- ledge, which in turn influences the students in their classes. When we serve teachers we are serving the cause of education, represented by the number of students who thereafter enroll in classes taught by them.

10. Opening up the panoramic view of libraries and their vast store-- house of knowledge must be done gradually or the patron is likely to be "turned off" from being overwhelmed.

11. The entire profession is enriched every time we can convince a student or faculty member that librarians are educators too, and that instead of being in opposition to one another, the two professions are a complement to each other.

The profession of librarianship moved along during the glorious age of the 1960s, when almost everyone who had any reason for concern about books, about library buildings, and about the preser-- vation of knowledge, was making himself heard. Sometimes there was a louder--than--usual clamor which seemed to reverberate throughout the halls of Congress. When President Kennedy intro-- duced the idea of knowledge and learning as a way of life for Amer-- ica, it was adopted as a major objective by many liberals and intel-- lectuals. Libraries began to emerge from their previous images as staid buildings maintained by the many for the benefit of the few into being a collection of everything known and available to every person with desires to make use of any kind of information to which he was inclined.

Now we seem to be losing our focus. We found that a long pe-- riod of frustrated desires did not cause neglected masses to converge on libraries. The dreams of making library services accessible to all the people, though not completely accomplished, were successful enough to prove that mere availability was not enough. Unless people really wanted libraries and the books therein, there was to be no mad rush. Though there had been a great increase in the desire for knowledge, libraries learned, to their dismay, that other media – newspaper, radio, television, private agencies, and even the telephone -- were filling a void which libraries, by not keeping up with the trends, were not filling. Many librarians began to realize that literacy does not necessarily result in book readers or library users. We now understand such terms as "literate illiterates." Schools, which we hoped would begin to turn out book lovers and library users, failed to do so.

College--bound young people turned out to be passive about li-- braries, though there were among them a large number of readers who relied upon the local bookstore or drugstore for their reading matter. The increased acquisition programs, helped largely by an in--put of federal funds, did not witness a concomitant or significant increase in library usage at all. The proliferation of printed materials in the guise of magazines, pamphlets, and books did not seem to in--crease the demand for information even among college professors. Instead, there seemed to develop what one famous historian referred to as an "anti--intellectual climate." Young people with unusual abilities sometimes became ashamed of receiving good grades, so found ways of reducing performance in order to make average grades. People seemed to become ashamed of knowing too much, so, as some critics believe, began to pass up opportunities for intellectual a-chievement. We came through a period when "egg head" was applied with scorn to the natural intellectual, and knowledge lost its flavor.

At this particular time in history, librarians are seeking ways to reverse the trend. During these two days you have been exploring ways of enticing young people, and faculty members, back into li--braries they have never really occupied. The fundamental belief is that if we can make them appreciate the tremendous resources avail--able in libraries, they will use them. We librarians believe that once one has developed a taste for learning, it will have a sort of narcotic effect on the person for life. Even more basically, we believe that when students know that libraries have all kinds of resources avail--able to them, and that librarians are there to help them ferret it out, they will, therefore, improve their intellectual skills by taking ad--vantage of the situation.

The question is, are we right in pushing for the intellectual de--velopment of students and faculty? Can we introduce information to young people in such a way that they become library users for life? Does a knowledge of resources actually help students to improve their learning, therefore their prospects? As librarians we would answer with a resounding yes. But how do we go about getting the financial resources from a non--intellectual public to bring about this type of program? How do we convince legislators that our cause is just? How do we sell the importance of library service to college administrators who often appear (to us, at least) to be anti--intellec--tual?

Though the answers to these questions cannot necessarily be answered in the same way for each individual, there are answers nevertheless. Each of you, believing in what you are trying to do, has journeyed here to try to ferret ideas from others which you can apply to your own campuses. You are the "salt", so to speak, of the intellectual world. Learning to you is important. You believe that the future of our society rests in its ability to continue to improve through learning. At least this is what I hope you believe. I would also hope that you believe in the dignity of the individual human being, and that every man is to be respected for what he is and for what he can contribute, no matter at what level the contribution is to be made. Who is to say that worthwhile ideas passed on to an in--dividual who may at this moment be just a freshman student will not help to produce a president, a senator, a great scientist, a community leader for the future?

During the past two months I have had the privilege of visiting three campuses where funded programs have induced orientation programs. This is not to say that nothing was being done previously, but the efforts of the Council on Library Resources have seemed to inspire greater impetus in these cases. I would point out to you that the programs in these three institutions have not yet been presented to the profession through printed reports. In each case, the librarians show dedication to their students and have been satisfied to make their contributions without a lot of fanfare. In other words, they are doing their own thing.

The first visit was to a small privately endowed, church--related institution in the city of New Orleans. Traditionally for black stu--dents, it now enrolls quite a few whites. The librarians, like many in such situations, do not have sufficient funds to provide proper re--sources for the ideal collection, nor are there enough professional staff for ALA standards. The funded program, however, enabled them to convince the administration and the faculty that students should know about libraries. They now teach one hour of a three--hour social science course required of all freshmen. In other words, the students attend the class two days a week for instruction in the social science subject and one day a week to receive help in finding course--related information. Each course requires a term paper, so the librarians assist students in developing note--taking techniques, the use of periodical indexes, developing bibliographies, and the use of the card catalog. Students who admittedly had little knowledge of library resources prior to enrollment appear quite vocal in their praise of librarians' efforts on their behalf. Since the entire pro--fessional staff is involved in the program, there is enthusiasm which was not as evident in other programs.

It is the enthusiasm of the librarians that makes that program effective. With too little administrative backing, they have a concern for students who must face tomorrow's world. Though the President of that institution has failed to find the matching funds, and the grant is subject to cancellation for that reason, the librarians state quite unequivocally that even if funding is withdrawn, they intend to go on with the program.

Another approach to the problem of orientation was demon--strated in a college in Mississippi. Since receiving CLR funds, they have been able to secure needed audio--visual materials for human--

ities courses. The program has captured the imagination of the faculty members to the extent that they rely upon libraries to intro–duce their students to the utility of the card catalog, note–taking, and writing papers. Librarians are invited into the classrooms where they present specially prepared bibliographies on subjects developed cooperatively with the teachers. The expertise of librarians is gaining recognition as they become immersed in educational prob–lems of students. Though this program is not yet reaching all of the students who need it, the number is growing. Most of 1,000 fresh–men who enter each year are soon made aware of the availability for library resources, and though they may not receive direct instruction, librarians report that they are getting many more inquiries or re–quests for help than before the program was begun.

The program in North Carolina has caught the imagination of most faculty members concerned with the humanities. Though the program is in its first year, one can sense that it has brought about some changes in attitudes about the library. During the first year, the concentration has been on teachers who are urged to utilize li–brary resources themselves, and to insist that students make use of them also. The failure of this program is that all librarians have not been involved in its structure. The enthusiasm of the young lady coordinating the program is only dimmed by her lack of admin-istrative support. The fact that the head librarian who wrote the proposal went on a leave of absence before the program actually started caused some problems, but these will be ironed out. The program is causing change on that campus and in that library.

It is not enough for any of you to rest upon your library school training. That was only a basis for action. As is pointed out in Alvin Toffler's *Future Shock,* change is taking place so fast that it is nec-essary to run fast in order to remain in the same spot. I hope that something you have obtained here will provide the impetus for you to use your imagination to innovate, and that meaningful improve-ments will emerge in the educational program of your campuses. It is not enough to be critical of what is not being done. If we are really to be the intellectual "salt" the country needs, we will do our best in our own way to improve tomorrow by affecting the lives of those who will be the instruments of a better society, and they will influence whether they learn a little or learn a lot. Throughout the entire learning process we are the leaveners whether we recognize it or not. Unless you have a sincere concern for other people as individual human beings, you are going to turn a lot of students off who need and want your help. You will have failed as an instrument to help that person achieve a better and satisfying life. Of course, I know that you will reflect this respect in your feelings and your service, and that you will go on being innovative and inventive. And from one librarian to another, God bless you for it.

BIBLIOGRAPHY ON LIBRARY ORIENTATION – 1973*

Hannelore B. Rader
Eastern Michigan University

Beede, Benjamin and Sandra Sadlow. "Reference Service: From Zero to Total Commitment," *RQ,* XIII (Winter, 1973), pp147-148.
Rutgers Law Libraries, when faced with the problem of providing library instruction for legal research, developed a three-phase program. First, they included library services information to all registrants; second, they provided the students with library tours; and third, they gave the students course-related library instruction by cooperating with the professors. Short guides to the literature were also prepared.

Bell, Caroline R. "Library for All, All for Library," *Journal of Reading,* XVII (November, 1973), pp119-121.
A high school reading teacher reports on her library skills experiment with slow and disabled readers to awaken their interest in the use of the library. With the cooperation of the media specialists it was possible to make the media center a learning center for the problem readers.

Benford, John Q. *Student Library Resource Requirements in Philadelphia.* Evaluation Report, Phase IV, June 15, 1971-June 30, 1972. Philadelphia: Philadelphia School District, 1972. ED 069294.
This is a report on Phase IV of the Student Library Resource Requirement Project—the Philadelphia School District. Major emphasis was on improvement of student reading skills, improvement of students' attitudes toward libraries and library materials, improvement of work study skills and increase of their knowledge about the community. Interviews, observation, and records were used to ascertain the situation. Related documents can be found under ED 057830, ED 057831, ED 060884, ED 060885.

Bichteler, Julie. "Self-Paced Instruction in Library Science—Second Thoughts," *Journal for Education for Librarianship,* XIII (Winter, 1973), pp188-192.
This article is an initial appraisal of the self-paced system of instruction used in a reference course in the Graduate School of Library Science at the University of Texas at Austin since 1971. Some of the

* Reprinted from *Reference Services Review*, v2 n1, January/March 1974, pp. 91-93.

inherent disadvantages of this type of instruction are pointed out. The conclusion reached suggests that a compromise between the self-paced and the traditional means of teaching would be the most advantageous.

Butterfield, Mary B. "Project LOEX Means Library Orientation Exchange," *RQ,* XII (Fall, 1973), pp39-42.
This article discusses the clearing house function and operation of Project LOEX located at Eastern Michigan University. The information so far collected by Project LOEX is summarized according to types and activities of orientation-instruction programs.

Carey, Robert. "Handling Information; a tape/chart course, an aid for teachers and librarians," *Education Libraries Bulletin,* XLVI (Spring, 1973), pp12-15.
This gives a description of a course for students to familiarize themselves with information in the university and college library. The course includes cassette tapes, transparencies, charts and a handbook, and was prepared and is used at Hatfield Polytechnic in Hertfordshire, England.

A Challenge for Academic Libraries. How to motivate students to use the library. Ed. by Sul H. Lee. Ann Arbor, Michigan: Pierian Press, 1973.
This work is comprised of the papers of the Second Annual Conference on Library Orientation held at Eastern Michigan University May, 1972. Mary Jo Lynch presents an overview of library instruction programs, Marvin Wiggins talks about a scientific model for the development of library instruction programs, Alice Cook reports on computer-assisted instruction in the use of libraries, and Charlotte Millis tells about student involvement in library orientation projects.

Collison, Robert. *30,000 Libraries: A Practical Guide.* Encino, California: Dickenson Publishing Co., Inc., 1973.
This book was written as a guide for the potential library user to make the most efficient use of the mass of materials contained within the more than 30,000 libraries in North America. It covers such areas as research, types of reference materials and the many offered services and facets of libraries. Appended are also some pictures of libraries, a list of types and titles of reference works, and an index.

Durey, Peter. "University Library Services to Undergraduates," *International Library Review,* V (July, 1973), pp321-327.
This article is concerned with providing instruction in library use for undergraduates in New Zealand Universities. It is mentioned that in Britain and the United States many bibliographic instructional programs exist. In addition, the author also discusses the importance of

the collection building to provide for the needs of the students and, secondly, the importance of making the collection accessable to the students.

Gruner, Charles R. "A Library-Research Assignment," *The Speech Teacher,* XXII (March, 1973), pp158-159.
This is a report of teaching freshmen the use of library resources through a basic speech course at the University of Georgia. The library assignment is described in detail and could be applied at other institutions.

Guidelines for Library Handbooks. Washington, D.C.: Federal Library Committee, 1972. ED 067137.
These guidelines are to assist in the preparation of printed materials to help the user find what he needs or wants as effortlessly as possible. The guidelines contain: information to be included in the hand-book, order of presentation, style of writing, format and design, and a list of supplemental reading.

Harrington, Jan. "SAM—Sources and Materials; IU's Undergraduate Library Course," *Focus on Indiana Libraries,* XXVII (Spring, 1973), p23.
This article reports on a library instruction program provided for undergraduates by graduate library science students at Indiana University. The graduate students involved receive degree credits for this project, and the undergraduates who received the instruction are unanimous in their appreciation for this service.

Heitert, Sylvia. "Card Catalog Teaching Aid," *School Library Journal,* September 15, 1973, p44.
A junior high teacher reports a successful and efficient way of teaching the card catalog use to new students in the seventh grade.

Kibbey, Ray A. and Anthony M. Weiner. "USF Library Lectures, Revisited," *RQ,* XIII (Winter, 1973), pp139-142.
This article describes the outreach approach to library instruction used at the University of South Florida. A library lecture series and a formal course on the library are offered there. A text for the course has been produced by the librarian teaching it. The outreach program has proven successful so far.

Kirk, Thomas. *Academic Library Bibliographic Instruction:* Status Report, 1972. Chicago, Ill.: Association of College and Research Libraries, 1973. ED 072823.
This report was authored by the Ad Hoc Committee on Bibliographic Instruction of the Association of College and Research Libraries. It contains in summary collected information about bibliographic in-

struction programs in 174 academic libraries in the United States. The programs were divided into four major categories: formal courses in library instruction; course-related library instruction; individualized library instruction; and other miscellaneous types of user instruction and orientation. Summarized tables of the actual programs are appended.

Kuo, Frank F. "A Comparison of Six Versions of Science Library Instruction," *College and Research Libraries,* XXXIV (July, 1973), pp287-90.
This is a report on a study to investigate the instructional effectiveness of six methods of library instruction in the Science Division of the Portland State University Library. The methods employed were: lecture, audiotape, slide-tape, television, and a combination of audiotape and discussion session. It was found that the most effective method of increasing student achievement on the ninety-item objective test designed to measure comprehension and retention of the content was the combination of the audio tutorial method followed by discussion sessions led by the librarian.

Larson, Paul M. *A Systems Approach to Individualized Library Instruction.* Fullerton, California: California State College, 1972. ED 071–681.
This study proposes individualized media library instruction based on an analysis of the library system. The slide-tape point of use modules exemplified in the study provide consistently needed instruction of high quality to individual users. Included is a 30-frame program for instruction to college library users in the use of periodicals. This report is a follow-up to ED 054765.

Nelson, Jerold. "Faculty Awareness and Attitudes Toward Academic Library Reference Services: A Measure of Communication," *College and Research Libraries,* XXXIV (September, 1973), pp268-275.
The results of a survey of faculties of six colleges indicate that the average faculty member is not aware of most services offered by the library. It is up to the libraries to promote available services and to provide these services consistently, competently, and vigorously. Communication between faculty and librarian must be initiated, mostly by the latter.

Palmer, Millicent. "Academic Library Instruction—Problems and Principles," *Tennessee Librarian,* XXV (Winter, 1973), pp11-17.
This paper was read at the annual meeting of the Tennessee Library Association, College and University Libraries Section on April 27, 1972 in Memphis. It discusses the many problems involved in providing effective library instruction to all students, and it gives many hints on how to go about the planning of such an instructional program.

Peele, David. "The Hook Principle," *RQ*, XIII (Winter, 1973), pp135-138.

Helpful hints are presented here to interest your faculty and students in a library lecture. Also provided are examples with which to start a library lecture, and to gain a captive and interested audience.

Saddler, Virginia B. *Role of the Library in Education; The Library Image as Presented in Selected Teacher Training Textbooks in Use in the State of Kentucky.* Barbourville, Ky.: Union College, 1970. ED 073789.

Questionnaires and examination of education textbooks used in basic introductory courses were the two methods used to determine educators' conceptions of the library and librarians. It was found that few of these textbooks included information on the library. A list of items that should be in a chapter on the library's role in public school education is included.

Schwartz, Philip J. *The New Media in Academic Library Orientation 1950-1972: An Annotated Bibliography.* Stout, Menomonie, Wisconsin: Wisconsin University, 1973. ED 071682.

This report presents a review of the literature in the area of media in academic library orientation from 1950-1972. Arrangement of the bibliography is by author and also by source to assist the reader searching the literature. Each entry in the latter part includes information as to the subject involved.

Sellmer, Donald Francis. *Teaching Fourth Grade Children to Use a Library Card Catalog: A Programmed Approach.* Ed. D. dissertation prepared at Ball State University, 1973.

The major purpose of this study was to find an effective method for elementary teachers and librarians to instruct their students in using the library as an educational resource. It was found in this study that a programmed text was more effective than a traditional instructional approach.

Show and Tell: A Clinic on Using Media in Library Instruction. Chicago, Illinois: American Library Association, 1972. ED 067841.

This catalog lists 45 exhibits shown at the ALA Conference Show and Tell Clinic in Chicago June 28 and 29, 1972, sponsored by the ALA Committee on Instruction in the Use of Libraries. These exhibits featured media and printed materials utilized by various types of libraries—public school, medical and academic—in order to instruct their users in the mechanics of library resources. (This item has a 1972 publishing date but did not appear in the ERIC form until 1973).

Stevens, Charles and others. "Library Pathfinders: A New Possibility

for Cooperative Reference Service," *College and Research Libraries,* XXXIV (January, 1973), pp40-46.
This article discusses the use of Pathfinders, originated at MIT, to introduce library users to the variety of information sources on particular topics available in research libraries. Pathfinders are like maps to the resources in a library, and it is their function to get the library patrons started on their information search. In MIT's Engineering Library the Pathfinders have proven to be effective time-savers for the users and the reference staff.

Stoffle, Carla J. and G. S. Bonn. "Academic Library Instruction in Wisconsin," *Wisconsin Library Bulletin,* LXIX (March-April, 1973), pp99-100.
This is a report of the Wisconsin Association of Academic Librarians workshop on academic library instruction held December 8, 1972 at the University of Wisconsin-Parkside. Comments are made on the difference between orientation and instruction as well as the various methods which can be utilized in library instruction.

Stoffle, Carla J. and G. S. Bonn. "An Inventory of Library Orientation and Instruction Methods," *RQ,* XIII (Winter, 1973), pp129-133.
This article reports on the status of library orientation-instruction in the state of Wisconsin. Information was collected at a state-wide workshop and from questionnaires. Types of instructional programs and methods of library instruction are discussed briefly, and it is concluded that the Wisconsin experience reflects nation-wide trends in the area of library instruction.

Vasilakes, Mary. "Video as a Service in Special Libraries," *Special Libraries,* LXIV (September, 1973), pp351-354.
The special library at the Westinghouse Electric Nuclear Center uses a closed circuit television system to train personnel. The involvement of the library in this area is growing, and the applications to instruction are discussed.

Yamada, Ken. "Instruction in the Effective Use of Library Resources," *Tennessee Librarian,* XXV (Winter, 1973), pp27-30.
This is a report on library orientation activities at Hiwassee College in Tennessee. An elective course on the "effective use of the library" was instituted there through the English department, and found quite useful by the students. Television and cassette tapes are also utilized to instruct students in the use of library resources.